# FAST FAB FOOD

*Other Books by Richard Cawley*

The New English Cookery

Not Quite Vegetarian

The Artful Cook

That's Entertaining

Easy Oriental

Outdoor Eating

Green Feasts

Ready Steady Cook 2

# FAST FAB FOOD

## Richard Cawley

HEADLINE

First published in 1997
by HEADLINE BOOK PUBLISHING

10 9 8 7 6 5 4 3 2 1

British Library Cataloguing in Publication Data
Cawley, Richard, 1947-
Fast fab food
1. Quick and easy cookery
I. Title
641.5'55
ISBN 0 7472 2098 0

**Cooking for photography** by Terry Farris
**Food photographs** by Anna Hodgson
**Illustrations** by Kate Simunek
**Designed** by Sara Kidd
**Edited** by Susan Fleming
ISBN 0 7472 2098 0

Typeset by Letterpart Limited, Reigate, Surrey
Printed and bound in Italy by Canale & C.S.p.A.

HEADLINE BOOK PUBLISHING
A division of Hodder Headline PLC
338 Euston Road
London NW1 3BH

*for*
*Angela Mason*
*a guiding star*

ACKNOWLEDGEMENTS

With many thanks to
**my mother**
who kept all the lights on and the front room door open. She danced
through life, laughing, and invited the world to join her party. I am very
grateful for having been at the top table.

And thanks also to
**Terry Farris**
for being a totally brilliant assistant and for cooking
the food for photography and making it look so wonderful
(and for being such fun to work with)
and
**Anna Hodgson**
for taking such stunning photos
(and also being such fun to work with)
and
**Susan Fleming**
my editor for understanding exactly what this book is all about

# CONTENTS

# INTRODUCTION — THE STORY SO FAR

### UNDER THE INFLUENCE

**Dad** Despite having managed by the age of eleven to have donned tights and greasepaint and sung 'It Was a Lover and His Lass' up a large *papier mâché* tree in an amateur production of *As You Like It* . . . my father still wouldn't let me train to be a ballet dancer.

Some years later, he resigned himself to my ambitions to become a fashion designer and gave his somewhat reluctant blessing when I (nearly sick with excitement and wearing my first pair of hipster flares) enrolled at my local art school, next to the gas works in Doncaster.

Eight years, four colleges and many many extraordinary outfits later, Dad (himself prone to a less than conventional suit) admitted fully to himself that I was not to become, like him, a civil engineer, and smugly basked in the reflected glory as I graduated from the illustrious Fashion School of the Royal College of Art with a Master's Degree 'with distinction', almost convinced that the whole thing had been his idea in the first place.

**Mum** Good food had always been a comfortable backdrop to my early 'glittering career'. My mother, a major influence, played two distinct roles, however. As the perfect cook and housekeeper she provided a home life of blissful reliable comfort and endless wonderful meals. But . . . when the lunch dishes were dried and put away, she would always change into an expensive frock and good shoes, become a 'lady' and (after 'just shutting her eyes for a few minutes') revel in the fruits of her early morning management. Always a believer in the 'all work and no play makes Jack a dull boy' adage, she spent her leisure hours in writing brilliant letters, gossiping, shopping, party planning and travelling to foreign parts.

She was always passionate about good food, and probably believed that, with gold shoes, it should

come on the National Health. I now realise that I take after her completely, but am more grateful for the legacy relating to the appreciation of good food, than the shopping and gold shoe bit!

She always cooked. Despite wash-day bad temper (due to her twin tub), her Monday shepherd's pie and rice pudding were faultless, her lamb chops were perfectly chosen and cooked to bone-gnawing perfection, whilst her mashed potato was better than that of any three-starred chef and (dare I say) perhaps even better than Delia's! Mum really came into her own, however, when it came to providing 'posh' food. She revelled in seasons of celebratory feasting. Our Christmas was always a lavish and fabulous affair. She would start months in advance making puddings, cakes and preserves; seeking out the best Valencia raisins; drying huge bunches of fresh marjoram for the stuffing; and gradually stocking our cupboards with every kind of tasty morsel, sweet and savoury. Her trifles were legendary, and she revelled in the compliments. Whilst not averse to a 'groaning board' she also well understood the merits of chic simplicity, and for my twenty-first birthday dinner party provided lobster salad followed by perfectly cooked roast fillet of beef.

Never conservative, she readily embraced new ingredients, changing food fashions and the influence of foreign travel and my precocious big sister (at college in London). Ours was surely the first family in Doncaster to eat real spaghetti, which come in a long blue packet (from London!) and was actually made in Italy.

Mum's dreams, I am sure, were filled with images of fresh sardines being grilled over charcoal in Portugal, freshly opened oysters eaten outdoors in a seaside restaurant in Brittany, and cellars filled with 'hanging' game, whole Stiltons and old port. In later years for birthdays we might receive through the post, not socks or aftershave, but smoked salmon from Ireland, smoked venison from Scotland, or perhaps even a tub of clotted cream from Cornwall.

One of the last meals she cooked for me began with a chic little salad of rocket and thinly sliced smoked duck breast dressed with her own home-made raspberry vinegar. A mother who, at the age of eighty odd, was still cooking trendy, slightly pretentious, but utterly delicious food, is a hard act to follow.

### TAKING UP THE CHALLENGE

At a very early age I already had pretentious ideas of my own about food. At nine I would walk into 'town' on Saturday mornings and sit alone, surrounded by middle-aged ladies in hats, and blow my whole week's pocket money on 'morning coffee' and an expensive cake. I must have presented a very odd sight, but I have never bothered about what other people thought and felt myself most sophisticated.

Some years later, after a year studying in Paris, I had acquired several new ideas well above my station and blush even now when I remember my first disastrous attempts at 'entertaining'. However, despite the odd culinary hiccough, including a strict macrobiotic diet (which I followed rigidly for almost a week), I never lost my passion for food, and rather than take up rugby, hang-gliding or some other energetic sport, cooking became my hobby and passion.

Through practice it seems I gained some skill in culinary matters, and after several years designing posh, expensive and fancy clothes for the rich, royal and famous, I won a cookery competition in a Sunday newspaper and almost overnight changed from a career in frocks to one in food.

Now, suddenly it seems, several more years have passed by. I have written loads of books, thousands of recipes for various magazines and newspapers, and cooked on all kinds of television programmes from making a chocolate and marshmallow pizza on Saturday morning children's television to my weekly spot on the ever popular

*Ready Steady Cook*, with new weekly appearances on *Can't Cook Won't Cook* and Channel 5's *Mixing It*. I have also managed to pack in an enormous amount of very varied travel, whether invited on 'press trips' by the various tourist boards or local food promotional agencies, or sent by magazines to write specific food stories, or on my own self-perpetuated trips to simply eat my way round the world. (More of this on page 23.)

Each recipe selected for *Fast Fab Food* had to fit simple criteria. It should be fast. Not just fast though, but fast and fabulous. This is a book for people who love food and want to cook, and while some recipes really do take only minutes to prepare and cook, there are others which require a bit more time and effort. There is nothing, however, which is difficult or fiddly and wherever possible, and where the end result will not suffer, any possible

short-cuts have been taken. White sauce, for example, is quick and easy with the fool-proof all-in-one method, and there are cake recipes which defy logic in their speed, ease of preparation and success rate.

All the ingredients in this book are available at large supermarkets, even those in the posher recipes. And whilst, in common with all serious cooks, I am obsessive about *always* using the best-quality ingredients (even if it is for making stock – only ever buy free-range chickens), I frequently make use of the huge range of excellent convenience foods and ingredients now available. (There is even a recipe on page 22 which consists of three packets, a tin and very little else!) Of course home-made stock is best (see page 101) but some cubes (Just Bouillon) are excellent, so don't be made to feel guilty by food writers who infer that using them makes you a dreadful person and 'not-a-serious-cook'.

A final but all-important thought about cooking my sort of 'fast food' is that it should be done slowly and thoughtfully, with love and pleasure, even if it is just a sandwich to be eaten alone. It will surely show in the end results, everyone will be a little bit happier and the world will be a better place.

*PS The twist to the end of this story (so far) is that, although I never managed to become a ballet dancer, this Christmas for a month I shall set aside my pots and pans and return to that wonderful world of greasepaint and tights in my first pantomime (in Canterbury). Watch this space!*

**Richard Cawley**

# CHAPTER 1

# SOMETHING IN THE FRIDGE

So you wake up from that Sunday afternoon nap in front of an old movie on the television, and there's no need to prepare dinner as there are plenty of leftovers from lunch if anyone feels hungry.

Oddly enough, though, you feel like cooking. Now, then, is the perfect time to rustle up something delicious which will provide you with gourmet treats for the next few days when you may have less time or inclination for 'proper' cooking. Apart from ending up with some totally yummy treat to store in your fridge (or a suitable airtight container), you will also be left with a lovely warm glow from having used your time so creatively.

Even so, these recipes are quick, easy and foolproof so you won't have to spend that long in the kitchen anyway, and there will still be plenty of the evening left to play back the second half of the movie you slept through earlier.

Oh, by the way, these recipes will work equally successfully if cooked on any other day of the week – if you happen to find a spare half hour or so and the urge to don a pinny.

# LEMON AND GARLIC CHICK PEA SPREAD

This works just as well with tinned cannellini or butter beans, and is the perfect low-cal. 'pâté' for snacking on at any time of the day – or night. Perfect just as it is on hot toast.

(SERVES 6)

1 x 420 g tin chick peas, drained
1 clove garlic, crushed
juice of 1 lemon
2 tbsp extra virgin olive oil
salt and pepper

▶ Reduce all the ingredients to a purée in a food processor, or mash thoroughly and mix with a fork. Transfer to a serving bowl, cover with kitchen film and refrigerate for up to 24 hours.

# AUBERGINE 'CAVIAR'

Variations on this dish are popular all over the Middle East, using different herbs and spices, and other flavourings. This is one of the simplest versions and quite delicious. You need to cook the aubergines over the open flame of a gas cooker or very close under a hot grill – or best of all over glowing charcoal. You will have to keep turning the aubergines until they are quite blackened on the outside and soft right through. This will take about 20 minutes. Poke a few holes in each aubergine first with a fork to prevent splitting.

(SERVES 6)

4 medium/large aubergines
3 tbsp extra virgin olive oil
2 cloves garlic, crushed
juice of 2 lemons
2 heaped tbsp chopped parsley
salt and pepper

to serve
extra olive oil
extra herbs

▶ Grill the aubergines (see above), cool slightly and carefully remove every trace of charred skins. Cut in half, then purée in a food processor.

▶ Transfer the purée to a sieve and press out as much juice as possible with the back of a spoon. Tip the purée into a bowl and whisk in the remaining ingredients, adjusting the seasoning as necessary. Transfer to a serving dish, drizzle with a little extra oil and garnish with a sprig of herbs. Chill for at least 2 hours (or up to 48) for the flavours to develop, but allow to come back to room temperature (about 1 hour) before serving.

▶ Serve with any kind of bread, toast, biscuits etc. Warm pitta is perfect.

# ROASTED CAPONATA

Caponata is a mixed vegetable dish from Sicily, and is a rather more exotic tasting cousin of the French dish Ratatouille. Here I have played fast and loose with the classic recipe, but the basic combination of ingredients remains the same, with the added robust, slightly caramelised flavour from roasting the vegetables instead of simmering them on top of the stove.

(SERVES 6 AS A STARTER, VEGETABLE COURSE OR VEGETABLE ACCOMPANIMENT)

2 level tbsp sultanas

25 g/1 oz pine kernels

6 tbsp extra virgin olive oil

5 tbsp red wine vinegar

3 tbsp sugar

2 heaped tbsp tomato purée

750 g/1 lb 10 oz aubergines, cut into approximately 2.5 cm/1 in cubes

4 sticks celery, cut into 1 cm/ ¹/₂ in lengths

1 large onion, roughly chopped

350 g/12 oz cherry tomatoes, left whole

salt and pepper

115 g/4 oz large green olives, stoned and chopped

1 heaped tbsp capers, drained

1 x 55 g tin anchovies, drained and chopped

2 heaped tbsp flat-leaved parsley leaves

▶ Soak the sultanas for an hour in a little hot water. Drain well.

▶ Preheat the oven to 200°C/400°F/gas 6.

▶ 'Toast' the pine kernels until golden in a hot dry frying pan.

▶ Whisk the olive oil with the vinegar, sugar and tomato purée in a large bowl, then add the aubergine, celery, onion and tomatoes. Toss well until every piece is coated.

▶ Transfer this to a roasting tin, spread out evenly and season well with salt and pepper. Roast in the oven for 40–45 minutes or until the vegetables are soft and beginning to brown at the edges.

▶ Remove from the oven and leave to cool to room temperature. Combine the remaining ingredients and stir these into the vegetables in the roasting tin. Transfer to a serving dish.

# MEDITERRANEAN VEGETABLE AND LENTIL BROTH

Make this chic, healthy and attractive main-course vegetable soup a day or two before and keep it in the fridge so that all you have to do thereafter is reheat it and serve it.

(SERVES 6)

1 tbsp extra virgin olive oil

1 onion, chopped

1 clove garlic, finely chopped

2 red or yellow peppers, deseeded and cut into bite-sized pieces

2 courgettes, sliced

2 leeks, trimmed and cut across into approx. 2 cm/$\frac{1}{2}$ in sections

3 sprigs thyme (or $\frac{1}{2}$ tsp dried)

1.5 litres/2$\frac{1}{2}$ pt chicken or vegetable stock (from cubes is fine)

1 x 400 g tin lentils, drained

salt and pepper

*to serve*

2 tbsp sesame seeds

► Heat the oil in a large lidded saucepan and stir-fry the onion over a medium heat for about 10 minutes, or until soft and transparent, adding the garlic halfway through.

► Add the peppers, courgettes, leeks and thyme, cover the pan and cook over the lowest possible heat, shaking the pan occasionally for 15 minutes. Add the stock and simmer uncovered for 20 minutes, then add the lentils and simmer for another 5 minutes. Season to taste with salt and pepper.

► Meanwhile, 'toast' the sesame seeds until golden in a hot dry frying pan.

► Serve the broth in hot bowls sprinkled with sesame seeds.

▲ Lemon and Garlic Chick Pea Spread. See page 14.

▲ Sally's Jelly Slice. See page 22.

# CURRIED COLESLAW

A variation on a well loved classic to jazz up your cold meats and sandwiches or just eat on its own. Add some shelled prawns and you have an unusual first course: add a few more and you have a delicious light meal.

(SERVES **6** GENEROUSLY)

**500 g/1 lb 2 oz white cabbage, finely shredded**

**1 large carrot, peeled and coarsely grated**

**1 red eating apple, cored and chopped**

**3 tbsp raisins or sultanas**

*the dressing*

**4 tbsp mayonnaise (your favourite)**

**4 tbsp natural yogurt (low-fat if you wish)**

**1 tbsp curry powder (your favourite), or more to taste**

**1 tsp sugar**

**juice of 1/2 lemon**

**salt and pepper**

▶ Make the dressing by mixing together the mayonnaise, yogurt, curry powder, sugar and lemon juice in a bowl.

▶ Season to taste with salt and pepper and stir in the cabbage, carrot, apple and raisins or sultanas.

# MEATLOAF 'EN CROÛTE'

You can make this without the pastry, but 'en croûte' it makes such a wonderfully economical and extremely substantial dish. Using bought pastry it is a doddle, and only needs an accompanying green vegetable or salad to provide a complete meal.

(SERVES 6)

500 g/1 lb 2 oz minced beef

500 g/1 lb 2 oz minced pork

2 onions, chopped

100 g/3½ oz brown
    breadcrumbs

1 tsp dried mixed herbs (Herbes
    de Provence if you have
    any)

2 free-range eggs, lightly
    beaten

1 tbsp Worcestershire sauce

salt and pepper

*the pastry*

1 large packet (370 g) puff
    pastry, thawed

1 egg yolk, mixed with 1 tbsp
    milk

▶ Preheat the oven to 180°C/350°F/gas 4.

▶ Combine the meats, onion, breadcrumbs and herbs. Add the beaten eggs, Worcestershire sauce and season with salt and pepper. Mix thoroughly and pack into a 900 g/2 lb loaf tin. Bake for 1½ hours. Loosen the loaf by running around the edges with a knife, then remove from the loaf tin, drain off any excess liquid and allow to cool.

▶ Roll out the pastry thinly to form a rectangle, place the meatloaf in the middle and wrap like a parcel, trimming off any excess. Place on a baking sheet with the 'seams' underneath.

▶ Decorate with pastry trimmings and brush with the egg glaze. Bake in a preheated oven at 220°C/425°F/gas 7 for 20–30 minutes or until puffed and golden.

▶ Serve hot, warm or cold.

# PORK, CHESTNUT AND APPLE PIE

Everyone loves a tasty meat pie. This one is unusual but very quick and easy to make. The recipe is based on a traditional one from the gloriously wild hills of the Cévennes in Southern France, close to which I am lucky enough to spend almost three months of the year.
Supermarkets now sell excellent vacuum-packed ready-peeled chestnuts. Use 450 g (1 lb) of the pastry for this pie, and keep the rest for another dish.

(SERVES 6)

*the pastry*
450 g (1 lb) plain flour
225 g/8 oz unsalted butter
2 egg yolks
6 tbsp cold water

*the filling*
1 tbsp extra virgin olive oil
200 g/7 oz onion, chopped
300 g/10½ oz lean pork (fillet is ideal), finely chopped
300 g/10½ oz eating apples, peeled, cored and finely chopped at the last minute
300 g/10½ oz cooked peeled chestnuts (see above), quartered
1 tbsp chopped fresh thyme (or ½ tbsp dried)
1 tsp chopped fresh sage (or ½ tsp dried)
salt and pepper
3 eggs
a little milk

▶ Make the pastry in your favourite way. I use a food processor. Chill for 1 hour. Preheat the oven to 200°C/400°F/gas 6.

▶ Heat the oil in a pan and stir-fry the onion over a moderate heat for about 10 minutes or until golden brown. Transfer to a bowl and mix in the pork, apples, chestnuts and herbs. Season to taste.

▶ Beat 2 of the eggs, add to the bowl and mix in well.

▶ Roll out two-thirds of the pastry and line the bottom of a non-stick, loose-bottomed, fluted 24 cm/9½ in flan tin. Fill with the pork mixture, smoothing it into a nice mounded shape.

▶ Roll out the rest of the pastry and make a lid, sealing the edges with a little water. Decorate the top of the pie with pastry trimmings. Beat the remaining egg with a little milk and use to glaze the pie. Bake for 40–50 minutes or until golden brown.

▶ Serve hot, warm or cold.

# FOOLPROOF LEMON YOGURT CAKE

This has to be the 'easiest cake in the world' and will give first-time success even to those who don't know one end of a wooden spoon from another. In fact it is a great cake to get children to bake.

Once you have mastered the basic recipe, you can change the flavourings (vanilla or coffee instead of lemon, for instance), the fillings (jam, whipped cream, mashed banana etc.) and be as fanciful with your topping as you like (candles will provide you with an ideal last-minute birthday cake).

You don't need to keep this in the fridge but an airtight tin will keep it moist for 2–3 days.

(MAKES 1 LARGE CAKE)
125 ml/4 fl oz natural yogurt
200 g/7 oz sugar
100 g/3½ oz butter, melted
2 small eggs
grated rind of 1 lemon
   (preferably unwaxed)
250 g/9 oz self-raising flour

*the filling*
1 x 325 g jar lemon curd (or to
   taste)

*the topping*
icing sugar

▶ Preheat the oven to 180°C/350°F/gas 4, and lightly oil and base line (with non-stick baking parchment or Bake-o-Glide) an 18 cm/7 in loose-bottomed or spring-form cake tin.

▶ In a large bowl whisk together the first five ingredients, then quickly but thoroughly beat in the flour. Pour into the prepared cake tin and bake in the centre of the oven for about 1–1¼ hours or until a skewer inserted in the centre of the cake comes out clean.

▶ Leave to cool in the tin for 10 minutes, then transfer to a cake rack to cool completely.

▶ Split in half to make two equal discs and then sandwich back together with the lemon curd. Dust the top with icing sugar or top with your favourite icing (icing sugar simply mixed with lemon juice would be perfect).

# CARROT CAKE WITH CREAM CHEESE FROSTING

This is the perfect carrot cake recipe (my bossy sister Christine gave it to me, so I have to say that). Simple to make and superb to eat.

(SERVES 6–8)

225 g/8 oz soft brown sugar

175 ml/6 fl oz vegetable oil

2 free-range eggs

grated rind of ¹/₂ orange

115 g/4 oz plain wholemeal flour

1 tsp bicarbonate of soda

1 tsp ground cinnamon

¹/₂ tsp ground nutmeg

225 g/8 oz grated carrot

55 g/2 oz chopped walnuts

*the frosting*

220 g/7 oz cream cheese

150 g/5¹/₂ oz icing sugar

▶ Heat the oven to 180°C/350°F/gas 4. Grease and line a 20–23 cm/8–9 in loose-bottomed cake tin with non-stick kitchen parchment.

▶ In a large bowl, mix together the sugar and oil with a wooden spoon, then one by one beat in the eggs. Beat in the orange rind.

▶ Sift the flour into another bowl with the bicarbonate of soda and the spices. Mix these dry ingredients into the sugar mixture, then quickly but thoroughly mix in the grated carrots and the nuts.

▶ Pour the batter into the prepared cake tin and bake in the centre of the oven for about 1 hour 10 minutes or until a skewer inserted into the thickest part of the cake comes out clean. Remove from the oven but leave in the tin to cool for 1 hour, then turn out on to a cake rack.

▶ Cream the frosting ingredients together and spread over the cake.

# SALLY'S JELLY SLICE

This recipe was given to me by a very good friend in Australia. It can be made in minutes and will disappear almost as quickly.

If you don't like the idea of using tins of condensed milk and packets of jelly don't make this recipe – however you will be missing out on something totally, totally gorgeous!

(MAKES **10–12** PORTIONS)

1 x 250 g packet Nice biscuits, crushed (a food processor is ideal)

100 g/3$^1$/$_2$ oz unsalted butter (no, don't use marge!), melted

*the middle layer*

1 sachet powdered gelatine (or the equivalent in leaf form)

175 ml/6 fl oz water

1 x 405 g tin condensed milk

juice of 2 lemons

*the topping*

1 packet strawberry jelly

300 ml/10 fl oz boiling water

150 ml/5 fl oz cold water

▶ Mix the crushed biscuits and melted butter and press into the base of a deep tin or dish. The shape or size doesn't have to be exact. (You could use a deep round quiche tin and then serve in wedges like cheesecake. I use either a square 'brownie' tin and cut in squares, or a 25 cm/10 in ceramic flan dish and cut in wedges.) Chill until set.

▶ Dissolve the gelatine in the water according to the instructions on the packet, then combine with the condensed milk and lemon juice. It will look curdled, but stir well and don't worry, it will set perfectly. Pour over the biscuit base and chill until set.

▶ Dissolve the strawberry jelly in the boiling water, add the cold water, stand until cool then pour over the lemon mixture and chill until set.

▶ Cut into individual portions (see above) to serve.

# CHAPTER 2

# THE GREEDY TRAVELLER

Travel has been one of the perks of my job. Press trips for instance, when a group of journalists are invited to visit a factory, farm, olive grove or even just a foreign country in the hopes that they will be so impressed that they will write a glowing report. There is a down side to these trips, however, as some factory visits can be terminally boring (plus the extremely unflattering paper hats and wellington boots worn to comply with hygiene regulations). The opportunity of a few days in Mauritius or Sweden learning about the local food (and drink), however, is not to be sneezed at (and wasn't).

Food writers are also sometimes sent abroad by their publications to write a particular story. For me this has involved hanging out of an open-sided helicopter in New Zealand to get good 'shots' of a fishing boat hauling in its nets; visiting coconut and tea plantations in Sri Lanka; making fresh pasta with an Italian granny outside Milan, and many other fascinating trips.

On my own initiative, I have 'enjoyed' a snake banquet in China and, in Japan (at the Tokyo Four Seasons Hotel, which has got to be one of the poshest hotels in the world – the loos even have heated seats!), among other weird and 'wonderful' delicacies, an exquisitely presented little dish of fish spermatozoa. Elsewhere in Japan, however, I ate a vegetarian banquet in a Buddhist temple which was perhaps the most beautifully presented and delicious meal I have ever experienced.

Or was my favourite meal the pumpkin curry on a tiny tropical island in the South China Seas? Or perhaps the marinated and barbecued lamb cutlets on the New Zealand sheep farm? Then again, for me, Australia has the best food in the world (I go every year to steal new ideas) . . .

Anyway, after all that 'hard work' and air-miles, here are just a few of my all-time favourite recipes from around the world.

# LAMB AND APRICOT TAGINE

On my recent first visit to Morocco I had the amazing good fortune to stay at La Mamounia. Like Raffles in Singapore and the Peninsula in Hong Kong, this glitzy art deco hotel is a legend in its own lifetime. Just outside the ancient walls of Marrakesh, it is hidden away behind its own towering mud-baked walls in a sumptuous 20-acre garden, an oasis of orange and olive trees and huge date palms.

Its guest list includes just about everyone who is or ever has been rich, royal or famous; Dietrich, Chaplin, St Laurent, the Stones, Caroline of Monaco, Elton John, Joan Collins (of course), Tom Cruise – and me!

Local casseroles are called tagines after the conical lidded pot in which they are cooked. My version, however, tastes excellent cooked in an ordinary lidded saucepan.

For a heartier feast serve this with 'instant' couscous from supermarkets, prepared in seconds according to the instructions on the packet.

(SERVES 6)

1 kg/2¼ lb boned cubed lamb (available in supermarkets)
2 onions, chopped
2 cloves garlic, crushed
2 tbsp extra virgin olive oil
1 heaped tsp ground cinnamon
1 heaped tsp ground ginger
1 tsp chilli powder (more or less to taste)
1 tsp ground cumin
1 tsp turmeric
1 tsp salt
3 heaped tbsp chopped fresh coriander
225 g/8 oz dried apricots (buy the no-soak kind)
1 heaped tbsp honey
2 x 420 g tins chick peas, drained
juice of ½ lemon (or more to taste)

*to garnish*
2 tbsp toasted flaked almonds

► Put the first 11 ingredients into a lidded saucepan with 850 ml/1½ pt water, bring to the boil and simmer for 1 hour.

► Add the apricots and honey and continue to cook for about another half hour or until the meat is tender and the apricots are swollen.

► Stir in the chick peas and the lemon juice (to taste), and continue to simmer for about another 5 minutes or until the chick peas are hot. Check the seasoning.

► Sprinkle with flaked almonds and serve with couscous (see above) or bread.

# CRUMBED PARSNIP AND PEAR SALAD WITH BLUE CHEESE DRESSING

Noosa is a very glamorous but relaxed beach resort in the 'Deep North' of Queensland. After a lazy day on a perfect white sand beach, the holiday-making glitterati are spoilt for choice when it comes to eating out. Of the many restaurants I sampled Anita's was my favourite, with a friendly relaxed atmosphere and the sort of fabulous simple food one comes to expect in Australia where the fresh ingredients are always of tip-top quality and need no more than the simplest preparation.

(SERVES 6)
6 medium parsnips, peeled
3 tbsp extra virgin olive oil
flour for dredging
2 eggs, lightly beaten
fresh white breadcrumbs
vegetable oil for deep-frying

the dressing
75 ml/2¹/₂ fl oz lemon juice
1 free-range egg yolk
75 g/2³/₄ oz Roquefort, Gorgonzola or your favourite blue cheese
1 heaped tsp chopped fresh tarragon (large supermarkets)
150 ml/5 fl oz vegetable oil
salt and pepper

to serve
1 bag prepared salad leaves (of your choice)
6 ripe pears, peeled, cored and sliced at the last minute
1 mild onion (red always looks nice), peeled and thinly sliced

▶ Preheat the oven to 180°C/350°F/gas 4.

▶ Rub the parsnips all over with the olive oil, arrange in one layer in a roasting tin and roast for 25–30 minutes until tender. Allow to cool, then quarter lengthways.

▶ Dip in flour, then egg, then breadcrumbs, shaking off the excess each time, and deep-fry in batches until crisp and golden. Drain on kitchen paper. Keep warm in a low oven once they are cooked.

▶ Meanwhile make the dressing by placing the lemon juice, egg yolk, cheese and tarragon in a food processor and blending until smooth. Then with the motor running drizzle in the oil to produce a thinnish mayonnaise-like dressing. Season to taste with salt and pepper.

▶ Put about a third of the dressing in a large bowl with the salad leaves and half the pear slices. Toss gently but thoroughly then pile the mixture into the centre of 6 plates. Pile the remaining pear slices, the onion and finally the fried parsnips on top, and then drizzle the remaining dressing over the salad and around the edge of the plates.

# SALT AND PEPPER PRAWNS

There are times when even those-who-never-get-tired-of-cooking feel like a night off, and I was thrilled when Penh An Chinese take-away opened close to my home in South London. Not only is it convenient, but it makes some of the best Chinese food I have ever tasted. So much so that when I recently celebrated a 'special birthday', I fed the sixty odd guests with Chinese take-away. This is one of my favourite dishes from Penh An and one of the ones I chose for my party. It is very quick to make and tastes fabulous. It also works brilliantly as a first course for a conventional western-style meal.

The quantities for the Chinese spiced salt are more than you need for this recipe, but it is great sprinkled on just about anything.

(SERVES **6** AS A FIRST COURSE OR PART OF AN ORIENTAL-STYLE MEAL)

**500 g/1 lb 2 oz large shelled raw prawns (thawed if frozen)**
**1 egg white, lightly whisked**
**1/2 tsp salt**
**2 tsp potato flour or cornflour**
**vegetable oil**
**1 clove garlic, thinly sliced**
**6 spring onions, sliced diagonally**
**2 chillies, deseeded and chopped (or more to taste)**
**1 tbsp sherry**

*the spiced salt*
**2 tbsp salt**
**1/2 tsp ground white pepper**
**1/2 tsp ground Sichuan peppercorns (or substitute ground black pepper)**

*to serve*
**salad leaves (bland crispy iceberg lettuce works well)**
**1/2 cucumber, deseeded and cut into small sticks**

▶ First make the spiced salt. Stir-fry the salt in a small non-stick pan over a medium heat for about 5 minutes or until it begins to darken slightly and become aromatic. Allow to cool then stir in the two kinds of pepper.

▶ Make an incision along the outer curve of the prawns and remove and discard any dark thread which might be there. Wash and dry thoroughly. Mix the egg white, salt and cornflour together in a bowl, add the prawns and mix thoroughly to coat.

▶ Heat about 5 cm/2 in oil in a wok until just beginning to smoke and then fry the prawns for about 30 seconds or just until they curl up and turn pink. They will not quite be cooked through at this stage. Transfer to kitchen paper with a slotted spoon and set aside.

▶ Remove all but about 2 tbsp oil from the wok and stir-fry the garlic, sliced spring onions and chilli over a high heat for 30 seconds. Return the prawns to the pan with 2 tsp of the seasoned salt, add the sherry, cover with a lid (an ordinary pan lid will do) and leave to cook for about 1 minute.

▶ To serve, arrange 'nests' of salad leaves and cucumber strips in the centre of 6 plates, then immediately spoon on the hot prawn mixture.

# AVOCADO, MANGO AND PRAWN SALAD

On one of my first visits to Australia I sampled this fabulous combination of ingredients. Australian avocados and mangoes are superb, and their prawns are justly legendary.

This recipe is quick to prepare, but you can do everything in advance if you like except for the avocados. Leave these to the last minute as once peeled they soon begin to discolour.

(SERVES **6**)

**1 large mango**

**2 avocado pears**

**350 g/12 oz shelled prawns**
   **(thawed if frozen)**

**¼ small red onion, finely**
   **chopped**

*the dressing*

**1 tbsp lemon juice**

**½ tsp sugar**

**salt and pepper**

**4 tbsp extra virgin olive oil**

**a few drops Tabasco sauce**

*to serve*

**a few salad leaves**

**1 tbsp chopped chives**

**lemon wedges**

**prawns in their shells (optional)**

▶ In a medium bowl, whisk together the dressing ingredients until well combined.

▶ Peel the mango and remove the stone as best you can. Cut the flesh into long thin slivers, and put in the bowl with any juices.

▶ Peel the avocados, remove the stones and cut the flesh across into thin slices. Put into the bowl with the shelled prawns and chopped red onion and toss all together as gently and thoroughly as possible. Try and make sure everything is coated in dressing without mashing up the avocado. Clean hands are by far the best tools for this job.

▶ Just before serving, arrange some salad leaves on 6 plates, dishes or bowls. Pile the prawn mixture on top, sprinkle with chopped chives and garnish with lemon wedges and shell-on prawns if using.

# MAURITIAN PINEAPPLE CHICKEN

Mauritius, way out in the Indian Ocean, has been colonised over the past 300 years with settlers from many parts of the world – India, Africa, France and China in particular – resulting in an extraordinarily varied and colourful cuisine.

Being lucky enough to visit this glorious tropical island, I managed to sample many of the different kinds of food, and discover how many of the exotic spices - which play such an important part in the local cooking - are grown on the island.

The food (we were staying in a pretty posh hotel) was fabulous. Particularly memorable was a special dinner for us visiting journalists. We were taken a little way along the coast in boats and deposited on a 'deserted' beach, where we sat under the stars at a magnificent white damask draped table, the silver and crystal glinting in the moonlight, and feasted on smoked local marlin, fresh palm hearts and gigantic freshwater prawns, grilled over charcoal. Under the table we wriggled our bare feet in the cool sand. A meal I shall never forget.

This adaptation of a spicy and fragrant Mauritian Creole dish will give you a little taste of that sunny spice island.

(SERVES 6)

6 chicken portions

salt and pepper

4 tomatoes

3 tbsp vegetable oil

1 onion, chopped

1 heaped tsp fresh thyme
     leaves (or $1/2$ tsp dried)

2 cloves garlic, crushed

1 tsp ground ginger

$1/2$ tsp ground cinnamon

a good pinch ground cloves

8 slices pineapple (tinned ones
     in natural juice are ideal)

150 ml/5 fl oz red wine (use
     white wine or chicken stock
     if you have no red wine)

▶ Season the chicken joints well all over with salt and pepper.

▶ Put the tomatoes in a bowl, and pour boiling water over them. Leave for a few seconds then drain. The skins should slip off easily.

▶ Heat the oil in a large lidded wok or sauté pan. (If your pan doesn't have a lid improvise with a double thickness of kitchen foil.)

▶ Fry the chicken over a low heat for about 7–8 minutes on each side or until golden, remove from the pan and reserve.

▶ Remove and discard all but about 1 tbsp of fat from the pan, then fry the onion gently in this with the thyme for 10–15 minutes or until soft and pale golden.

▶ Add the garlic and spices to the onion for the last

couple of minutes, stirring them in well.

▶ Meanwhile purée 2 drained pineapple slices (reserve the juice for another use) with the tomatoes and wine in a food processor or liquidiser, then season with a little salt and pepper.

▶ Pour half the pineapple mixture into the frying pan and arrange the chicken pieces, skin side up, on top.

▶ Pour the remaining pineapple mixture over the top of the chicken and cover the pan with a lid (see above). Simmer gently for 20–30 minutes until the chicken is really tender.

▶ Just before serving arrange 4 more slices of pineapple on a foil-lined grill pan and cook under a preheated grill for 2–3 minutes each side or until just beginning to turn brown at the edges. Watch them carefully as they burn easily.

▶ Arrange the chicken on hot plates. Spoon over the sauce from the pan and top with the grilled pineapple rings.

▶ Serve with plainly cooked white rice and fresh green vegetables or salad.

# GRAVAD LAX WITH DILL SAUCE

During a recent fabulous trip to Sweden to find out about the excellent products they are now importing to England, including their superb pork, I spent a day as a 'student' in the super-modern Department of Restaurant and Culinary Arts in the University of Örebro, where I was taught this classic Swedish recipe by top chef Per Gustafson.
The recipe differs somewhat from others I have seen, but is the best I have tasted. It is very easy to make with perfect results if, like I did, you follow Per's recipe to the letter.

(SERVES 6 OR MORE AS A FIRST COURSE)
500 g/ 1 lb 2 oz fresh skin-on salmon fillets (in 2 even-sized pieces)
250 g/9 oz sugar
125 g/4¹⁄₂ oz salt
¹⁄₂ tsp white peppercorns, crushed (use a mortar and pestle if possible)
25 g/1 oz fresh dill (including stalks)

the sauce
2 heaped tbsp Dijon mustard
1 tbsp sugar
200 ml/7 fl oz sunflower, corn or other tasteless vegetable oil
salt and white pepper
3 tbsp chopped dill fronds (chopped at the last minute, and only once or it becomes bitter)

▶ Start the sauce the day before required. Put the mustard and sugar in a processor or blender (a hand-held wand-type is perfect) and, with the motor running, add the oil in a thin steady stream to produce a rather translucent, mayonnaise-like sauce. Season to taste with salt and pepper and refrigerate until an hour or two before needed. Remove from the fridge and stir in the dill.

▶ To cure the salmon, mix together the sugar, salt and crushed pepper and rub all over the salmon. Chop the dill fronds and crush the stems with a rolling pin or bottle.

▶ Arrange one piece of the salmon, skin side down in a shallow dish, cover with about two-thirds of the dill and sprinkle over any remaining sugar mixture. Put the other piece of salmon on top, skin side up to make a sandwich and sprinkle over the remaining dill. *Leave at room temperature for about 2 hours,* then refrigerate for 12–24 hours, turning over occasionally and basting with any juices which seep out. *Do not* weight the fish as most recipes suggest, as this squeezes out precious juices and makes the flesh much harder.

▶ To serve, scrape off the sugar mixture and dill, slice as thinly as possible on the diagonal, and serve as you would smoked salmon, with the sauce and perhaps a simple cucumber salad dressed with a little vinegar.

# SPAGHETTI ALLE VONGOLE

The meal I choose with boring regularity when eating in Italy is Spaghetti alle Vongole followed by Fritto Misto di Mare (mixed deep-fried seafood), followed by a simple green salad – perfection.

As it is unlikely in this country to find fresh clams use the excellent tinned ones sold in delicatessens. John West Baby Clams are ideal.

In this recipe I save some of the tomatoes to add to the sauce right at the end to give a pleasant sharp fresh taste to the rich sweet flavour of the cooked tomatoes in the sauce.

(SERVES **6** AS A SUBSTANTIAL STARTER OR LIGHT MAIN COURSE)

**450 g/1 lb spaghetti, cooked according to the instructions on the packet and drained**

*the sauce*
**3 tbsp extra virgin olive oil**
**1 onion, chopped**
**3 cloves garlic, chopped**
**1 tsp dried oregano**
**$\frac{1}{2}$ tsp dried thyme (or 1 tsp fresh)**
**4 tbsp Italian dry vermouth (the more aromatic and herby the better)**
**600 g/1 lb 5 oz very ripe tomatoes, roughly chopped**
**1 x 290 g tin clams, drained**
**salt and pepper**

*to garnish*
**small basil leaves (optional)**

▶ Heat the oil in a large saucepan and stir-fry the onion over a low/medium heat for about 10 minutes or until quite soft and transparent but not browned. Add the garlic and herbs and cook stirring for another 5 minutes. Do not allow the garlic to brown.

▶ Add the vermouth and allow it to bubble for a couple of minutes until almost evaporated, then add about two-thirds of the tomatoes. Cover the pan and simmer for 10 minutes. Remove the lid and add the clams and remaining tomatoes. Season with salt and pepper. Cover the pan and continue to cook, shaking the pan occasionally for 2–3 minutes or just until the clams are heated through.

▶ Pour the sauce over the cooked pasta, mix together and divide between 6 warmed soup plates. Garnish with basil leaves if using and serve at once.

# GRILLED POLENTA WITH PRAWNS

I ate this in the hot spring sunshine of Venice in a heavenly restaurant called the Ponte del Diavolo on the edge of a perfect daisy-carpeted orchard on the island of Torcello.

At the restaurant the dish is prepared with local fresh raw prawns which have the most wonderful flavour. Unfortunately the only kind of uncooked prawns we can buy in this country are from tropical waters. These are fine in spicy dishes like Thai curries, but don't have enough flavour to add to a simple dish like this. Therefore buy medium-sized cooked prawns with the shells on from the fishmonger and remove the shells yourself (these make excellent fish stock!). They will probably have come from cold waters and have masses of flavour.

(SERVES 6)

1 x 200 g/7 oz packet instant polenta (the kind which cooks in 5 minutes – available from supermarkets and delicatessens)

50 g/1³/₄ oz Parmesan cheese, freshly grated

salt and pepper

extra virgin olive oil

1 clove garlic, sliced

shell-on prawns (see above), shelled (allow about 12-14 per person)

2 tbsp finely chopped parsley (the flat-leaved kind if possible)

juice of ¹/₂ lemon

▶ Cook the polenta according to the instructions on the packet, adding the cheese just before it is done, and then pour into an oiled 20 cm/8 in pie dish. Allow to cool. It will set solid.

▶ Remove the polenta from the dish and cut into 6 even wedges, like a cake. Season and brush these all over with olive oil and then grill until golden brown and crispy on both sides. This will take longer than you would expect, about 3–4 minutes each side depending on the heat of your grill. You can also do this on a heavy cast-iron ridged 'grill' frying pan. Keep hot.

▶ Meanwhile heat 6 tbsp olive oil in a small pan and add the garlic. Cook over a moderate heat until the garlic is golden brown. Remove garlic with a slotted spoon and discard.

▶ Add the prawns, parsley and lemon juice to the oil and season with salt and pepper. Cook for another minute, shaking the pan, or just until the prawns are hot. Do not overcook or they will become tough.

▶ Place a wedge of grilled polenta on each of 6 heated plates then spoon over the prawns and flavoured olive oil. Serve immediately.

▲ Crumbed Parsnip and Pear Salad with Blue Cheese Dressing. See page 25.

▲ Salt and Pepper Prawns. See page 26.

# Sri Lankan Chicken Curry

I learnt how to make this wonderfully aromatic curry on a trip to the stunningly beautiful island of Sri Lanka.

The ingredient list is long, but you will probably already have many of the ingredients in your store-cupboard, and once assembled the recipe only takes minutes to prepare. Creamed coconut is available in most large supermarkets and Asian grocers.

(SERVES 6)

6 chicken portions

*the marinade*

2 tsp chilli powder

1/2 tsp turmeric

1 tsp ground coriander

1 tsp salt

1 large clove garlic, crushed

1 tsp finely chopped fresh
   ginger

4 cloves

5 whole cardamom pods

2.5 cm/1 in stick cinnamon

1 fresh green chilli, chopped
   (include seeds if you like
   hot curry)

1 large tomato, chopped

*the curry*

1 tbsp ghee, clarified butter or
   vegetable oil

1 onion, chopped

2 bay leaves

1/2 tsp fenugreek seeds

450 ml/16 fl oz water

50 g/1¾ oz (¼ block) creamed
   coconut, chopped

1 tbsp lime juice

1 scant tsp sugar

1 heaped tsp curry powder

▶ Put the chicken pieces in a large bowl with all the marinade ingredients and mix very thoroughly. Cover with kitchen film and leave for at least 2 hours, but preferably overnight.

▶ Heat the ghee, butter or oil in a large lidded pan or wok and stir-fry the onion and bay leaves over a medium heat for about 5–10 minutes or until the onion is golden. Add the fenugreek and continue to stir-fry for about another 30 seconds.

▶ Add the chicken and marinade ingredients with the water, bring to the boil, cover the pan and simmer gently for 15–20 minutes or until the chicken is tender.

▶ Add the creamed coconut and stir until dissolved, then stir in the lime juice, sugar and curry powder and simmer for only 1 minute longer.

▶ Serve with boiled rice, poppadoms and any salads, sambals or chutneys you fancy.

# CESAR SALAD

This is one of those classic dishes with as many 'authentic' recipes as restaurants who serve it. This one was given to me by my friend Martha Holmberg, who is a successful American food writer and editor. It might not pass muster with purists, but it contains all the essential ingredients, is a cinch to make, and very good to eat.

(SERVES 6)

**1 large head of cos or romaine lettuce (no other kind will really do)**

*the dressing*

**1 free-range egg yolk**
**3 tbsp lemon juice**
**$^1/_2$ tsp Dijon mustard**
**1 clove garlic, crushed**
**6 anchovy fillets, drained**
**a dash Worcestershire sauce**
**pepper**
**125 ml/4 fl oz extra virgin olive oil**

*the croûtons*

**3 tbsp extra virgin olive oil**
**1 clove garlic, sliced**
**3 slices white bread, cut into 1 cm/$^1/_2$ in cubes**

*to serve*

**100 g/3$^1/_2$ oz Parmesan cheese, freshly grated**

▶ Discard any coarse or damaged outer leaves of the lettuce. Wash the rest and dry thoroughly then tear into bite-sized pieces and put in a serving bowl.

▶ To make the dressing put the egg yolk, lemon juice, mustard, garlic, anchovies and Worcestershire sauce in the bowl of a food processor or liquidiser, and season to taste with pepper. You should not need to add extra salt as the anchovies contain enough. Process until smooth and then add the oil in a thin steady stream until well blended. It will look like a cross between a mayonnaise and a thick vinaigrette. Season.

▶ To make the croûtons, heat the oil in a large frying pan (a wok is ideal if you have one). Fry the garlic over a medium heat until golden brown then remove and discard. This will have flavoured the oil. Fry the cubes of bread in the garlic oil, stirring constantly until crisp and golden. Drain on kitchen paper and allow to cool.

▶ Pour the dressing over the lettuce and toss well, sprinkle over the croûtons and Parmesan and serve at once.

# CHINESE-STYLE BRAISED LEG OF LAMB

I adore oriental food of all kinds but this recipe is my own adaptation of a classic Chinese recipe for braised duck.

As lamb has a texture and strong flavour not dissimilar to duck it works very well in this recipe, is easily available and considerably cheaper.

I like to serve this lamb in an East-meets-West style meal with stir-fried vegetables and plainly cooked basmati rice.

(SERVES 6)

1 leg of lamb, about 1.8 kg/4 lb

*the braising liquid*

1 x 5 cm/2 in piece each of lemon and orange peel

2 cloves garlic, crushed

350 ml/12 fl oz Kikkoman soy sauce (undoubtedly the best)

3 tbsp rice or white wine vinegar

150 ml/5 fl oz dry sherry

2 tbsp dark brown sugar

4 spring onions, cut into 5 cm/ 2 in pieces (include good green parts)

4 x 5 mm/¼ in slices unpeeled fresh ginger (exact quantity isn't crucial)

6 star anise (supermarkets)

1 x 5 cm/2 in stick cinnamon

450 ml/16 fl oz water

▶ Preheat the oven to 200°C/400°F/gas 6.

▶ Arrange the lamb in a lightly oiled lidded casserole dish, or if you haven't one large enough, use a deep ovenproof dish or roasting tin and improvise a 'lid' with a double layer of kitchen foil.

▶ Put all the braising liquid ingredients in a saucepan and bring to the boil. Pour over the lamb, cover the casserole/dish/pan and cook in the oven for 15 minutes. Turn down the heat to 150°C/300°F/gas 2, and continue to cook for another 2¼ hours. Turn the lamb occasionally, basting with the liquid, to ensure that it cooks evenly.

▶ Remove the lamb and set aside in a warm place to rest for 15 minutes. Strain the cooking liquid into a large saucepan, discarding the solids. Boil hard until reduced by half. This will make a very intensely flavoured 'gravy'. Serve separately in a sauceboat.

▶ Carve as you would a roast leg of lamb.

# GRILLED GOAT'S CHEESE SALAD

In the South of France where I spend almost a quarter of my year, goat's cheese is a speciality and all the markets have at least one stall selling 'chèvres'. These vary from day-old cheeses – chalky white, creamy and bland, still dripping whey from their perforated plastic containers – to hard little, dry, dark-coloured discs with a distinctive strong flavour and acrid smell. The fresh ones make wonderful puddings served drizzled with lavender honey or topped with a blob of sweetened chestnut purée, whilst the older ones are definitely an acquired taste.

The cheeses which are a few days old, still pearly white and slightly firm, are ideal for this recipe.

(SERVES 6)

3 slices brown bread

6 small medium firm goat's
    cheeses (see above), or
    6 x 1 cm/½ in slices from
    the kind which comes in a
    log (in most supermarkets
    and delicatessens)

1 bag mixed salad leaves (your
    favourites)

extra virgin olive oil

black pepper

▶ Cut circles from the bread, a fraction larger than the cheeses and toast on one side.

▶ Sit the cheeses on the untoasted side and grill until beginning to melt and brown. (If you haven't got access to a grill, you can toast the bread and grill the cheeses separately on a barbecue very successfully.)

▶ Make 'nests' of leaves on six plates, place a circle of toast and cheese on each, drizzle with oil, sprinkle with pepper and serve at once.

# SOUPE AU PISTOU

Another favourite recipe from the South of France, this chunky minestrone-like main-course soup reputedly originated in Nice. It is unusual in that its main flavouring, the 'pistou' – named after the pestle with which the pungent paste of basil, garlic and olive oil, with perhaps cheese was pounded – is stirred in at the last minute. Just over the Italian border from Nice, Liguria is famous for its 'pesto' sauce, an almost identical preparation. Excellent ready-made pesto is available in most delicatessens and supermarkets, and works perfectly for this recipe.

In summer when vegetables are at their peak, Diane, a kind neighbour (who also waters our treasured wisteria), always makes us an enormous panful, which tastes like distilled summer. This is my recipe, which tastes almost as good.

**(SERVES 6 AS A MAIN COURSE)**
**175 g/6 oz dried beans (I use**
   **¹/₂ red kidney and**
   **¹/₂ white cannellini)**
**1 onion, chopped**
**2 leeks, sliced**
**2 carrots, diced**
**2 potatoes, peeled and diced**
**2 sticks celery, chopped**
**500 g/1 lb 2 oz green beans**
   **(any kind), cut into 1 cm/**
   **¹/₂ in pieces**
**500 g/1 lb 2 oz tomatoes,**
   **chopped**
**350 g/12 oz courgettes, sliced**
   **or diced (depending on size)**
**100 g/3¹/₂ oz macaroni or other**
   **small pasta shapes**
**salt and pepper**

*to serve*
**4 tbsp ready-made pesto sauce**
**fruity extra virgin olive oil**

▶ Soak the dried beans in cold water for 12 hours, then drain.

▶ In a large saucepan, simmer the soaked dried beans in 1.75 litres/3 pt unsalted water for 1 hour or until tender. Drain and return to the pan.

▶ Add the onion, leek, carrot, potato and celery. Cover with 2.25 litres/4 pt water, bring to the boil, then simmer for 20 minutes. Add the green beans and tomatoes and continue to simmer for 10 minutes. Add the courgettes and pasta, season with salt and pepper and continue to cook for about 15 minutes more or until the pasta is tender.

▶ To serve, thin the pesto with a ladleful of the hot soup liquid in a serving jug.

▶ Ladle the soup into heated dishes. Each guest adds as much of the 'pistou' as he likes and perhaps a drizzle of olive oil.

# PAVLOVA

This gorgeous gooey confection of meringue and cream, named after the famous ballerina on a trip 'down under', is always a sure-fire success as a spectacular party pudding. You can use whatever fruit you fancy for a topping, but the classic Aussie combination is strawberries and passionfruit.

(SERVES 6-10)
*the pavlova*
4 free-range egg whites
a pinch salt
250 g/9 oz caster sugar
2 tsp cornflour
1 tsp vinegar

*the filling and topping*
300 ml/10 fl oz double cream, whipped
200 g/7 oz strawberries, hulled and halved
the juice and pulp from 4 passionfruit

▶ Preheat the oven to 150°C/300°F/gas 2.

▶ Beat the egg whites and salt until light and fluffy, then whisk in the sugar gradually, and continue to whisk until the mixture is stiff and glossy. It is important that all the sugar is dissolved at this stage or the meringue will 'weep' when cooked. If in doubt rub a little of the mixture between the fingers and you will soon feel if there are still undissolved sugar granules.

▶ Fold the cornflour and vinegar into the meringue mixture.

▶ Spread the meringue on to a non-stick baking parchment lined baking sheet in a circle measuring about 23 cm/9 in across.

▶ Place in the preheated oven and immediately turn the temperature down to 140°C/275°F/gas 1 and cook for 1¼ hours. Remove from the oven and allow to cool completely.

▶ Remove the meringue from the sheet and carefully peel off the paper.

▶ Transfer the pavlova to a serving plate and just before serving pile on the cream then the strawberries and finally drizzle over the passionfruit juice and pulp.

# CHAPTER 3

# GOLDEN OLDIES

Food fashions come and go, and over recent years trends seem to change almost as quickly as those in clothes.

Take ingredients, for example. One minute it's kiwi fruit with everything from duck to fish cakes, and the next minute we would die rather than put so much as a slice in a fruit salad. We've recently had rather a surfeit of the sun-dried tomato. It's delicious, of course, but less versatile, if anything, than the poor old kiwi, yet it has found its way into every manner of sauce, stuffing, salad and pretty well anywhere it can squeeze.

It's all so confusing, as the merry-go-round whirls faster and faster. Did salsas replace coulis? Should we be serving mashed potato with some trendy additive such as olive oil and garlic instead of butter (chopped sun-dried tomato or kiwi fruit might be different?), or should we be sitting everything on a bed of oh-so-trendy (but not that delicious) couscous. And just when we have mastered the art of grilling polenta, we notice that all the trendiest restaurants are serving 'soft' polenta.

Be a bit of a rebel, like me, and occasionally turn a blind eye to food fashions. Cook exactly what you fancy and exactly what you want to eat. Fish pie and lamb chops with mash might not exactly be hot news for foodies, but my, are they good to eat. Spag. Bol. might be on every ordinary pub and caff menu but it's certainly delicious (particularly if you use my recipe). And like the Chanel suit, a really good prawn cocktail is well worth a revival.

So, turning a blind eye to fads and trends, here is my selection of decidedly unfashionable but irresistible recipes: old favourites and the odd French classic (remember French food?) with the occasional Cawley twist to get them ready for the twenty-first century.

*PS Spot the sun-dried tomatoes!*

# PRAWN COCKTAIL

 There was a time when this much bastardised recipe appeared on the menu of almost every provincial English restaurant – and was, at its worst, a very nasty concoction of shredded, wilted lettuce, watery tinned shrimps and a horrid pink, chemical-tasting sauce. Made with good-quality ingredients, however, nothing could be nicer for a simple, easy-to-make first course, particularly with the modern addition of sun-dried tomatoes which I have snuck into the classic recipe.

(SERVES 6)

675 g/1½ lb medium cooked peeled prawns (see page 32), thawed and well drained if frozen

*the sauce*

1 tbsp tomato ketchup

1 tbsp very finely chopped sun-dried tomatoes or sun-dried tomato paste

2 tsp Worcestershire sauce

2 tsp lemon juice

a few drops Tabasco sauce (to taste)

½ tsp dry English mustard

a pinch salt

3 tbsp lightly whipped cream

*to serve*

approx. 50 g/1¾ oz baby salad leaves (add a bit of rocket if you have any)

6 large shell-on prawns

6 lemon slices

► First make the sauce. Thoroughly mix together the first 7 ingredients in a small bowl, then fold in the whipped cream.

► Just before serving divide the salad between 6 large stemmed wine glasses. Scatter over the peeled prawns, and drizzle over the sauce.

► Garnish the rim of the glasses with the lemon slices and large shell-on prawns.

# MOULES À LA MARINIÈRE

Many people choose this in restaurants but are afraid to cook mussels at home. Follow these instructions and you will realise how quick and easy it is. Most mussels now come ready cleaned in 1 kg/2¼ lb bags. If not you must first scrape away any barnacles with a sharp knife, then scrub the shells very thoroughly under cold running water. Next strip away any 'beard' which protrudes from the join in the straight side of the shell and again rinse in cold running water.

The mussels should then be soaked in cold water for at least an hour to remove any traces of dirt or sand. Change the water at least three times. Drain the mussels and give any which remain open a sharp tap. If they still remain open they are dead and must be thrown away. Also discard any which seem cracked or dubious.

(SERVES 6)

1 medium onion, chopped

2 shallots, chopped (if not available add another medium onion)

2 cloves garlic, chopped

2 tbsp chopped parsley

300 ml/10 fl oz dry white wine (the one you will be drinking with the meal)

2 kg/4½ lb mussels, cleaned as above

juice of ½ lemon

salt and pepper

50 g/1¾ oz best unsalted butter

▶ Put the onion, shallot (if using), garlic, half the parsley and the wine in a large heavy-bottomed saucepan, bring to the boil, turn down the heat and simmer for 5 minutes. Add the mussels and cook for 3–4 minutes, shaking the pan occasionally. Do not overcook or they will become rubbery. Remove the mussels to a serving dish, discarding any that refuse to open, cover and keep warm.

▶ Strain the cooking liquids into another pan (I usually don't bother, as I like to keep the bits of onion and shallot – even if there is the tiniest bit of sand left in the sauce). Reheat, adding the lemon juice and seasoning with salt and pepper. Stir in the butter until melted and pour the sauce over the mussels.

▶ To serve, sprinkle over the remaining parsley and serve immediately with lots of French bread and cold white wine. A good tip is to eat the mussels the way many of the French do, and that is to use an empty mussel shell (hinged pair that is) as a pair of pincers to remove meat from the shell and transfer it to your mouth neatly and efficiently.

# FISH PIE

A classic fish pie topped with fluffy mashed potatoes is the ultimate comfort food, and quick and easy to make if you use the all-in-one method for the white sauce.
The fish suggested is merely a guideline – you can use any firm fish you want.

(SERVES 6 AS A MAIN COURSE)

1.5kg/3 lb 5 oz old potatoes, peeled

salt and pepper

1 kg/2¼ lb prepared fish (e.g. halibut, salmon and smoked haddock fillets)

1 bay leaf

1 strip lemon peel

1-2 sprigs parsley

1-2 sprigs dill (optional)

150 ml/5 fl oz dry white wine

600 ml/1 pt full-fat milk

2 level tbsp flour

50 g/1¾ oz butter

100 g/3½ oz shelled prawns (thawed if frozen)

2 hard-boiled free-range eggs, roughly chopped

1 heaped tbsp finely chopped parsley or dill

50 g/1¾ oz unsalted butter, cut into small pieces

▶ Preheat the oven to 200°C/400°F/gas 6.
Cook the potatoes in boiling salted water until tender, then drain and mash, seasoning well.

▶ Meanwhile put the fish fillets in one layer, skin side down, in a large lidded frying pan (a lid can be improvised with a plate or foil) with the bay leaf, lemon peel and the sprigs of parsley and dill (if used). Pour over the wine and cook covered over a low heat for about 10 minutes or until the fish is just cooked through.

▶ Transfer the fish to a plate with a fish slice, then strain the pan juices into a clean bowl, discarding the aromatics. Discard the fish skin and break the flesh into large flakes.

▶ While the fish is cooking make the white sauce, by putting the milk, flour and butter – all cold – into a small saucepan and bring to the boil slowly, whisking constantly, then simmer over the lowest possible heat (a heat diffuser is a good idea) for 10 minutes, stirring frequently. Add the reserved fish cooking juices to the sauce and season to taste with salt (go steady if including smoked fish which is already quite salty) and pepper.

▶ Transfer the sauce to a bowl and gently fold in the cooked fish, prawns, eggs and chopped herbs. Spoon the mixture into a greased shallow ovenproof dish, cover with the potato and dot with the butter.

▶ Bake for about 30 minutes or until piping hot and the potato topping has begun to brown in places. Pop it under a hot grill at the last minute if you like.

# FISH IN BEER BATTER AND CHIPS

Fish fried properly in crisp batter is undoubtedly one of the great culinary classics of the world – and perhaps best served in Yorkshire fish and chip shops.

Any fresh fillets of fish will do but for an up-market version take advantage of the excellent trout fillets now available in many supermarkets (but be sure to remove any fine bones before cooking).

This easy and foolproof batter is best made at the last minute.

Deep-frying, however, needs plenty of last-minute concentration, so I cook my 'chips' in the oven. Olive oil is the best for flavour.

(SERVES **6**)

*the fish*
**175 g/6 oz plain flour or more as necessary**
**approx. 250 ml/9 fl oz lager**
**6 fish fillet portions (see above), each weighing approx. 250 g/9 oz**
**vegetable oil for deep-frying**

*the chips*
**1 kg/2¼ lb old potatoes, peeled and cut into very chunky chips or wedges**
**6 tbsp extra virgin olive oil**
**salt (Maldon if possible)**

*to serve*
**malt vinegar (or lemon wedges if you are feeling poncey)**
**ketchup or tartare sauce (optional)**
**parsley sprigs**

▶ Preheat the oven to 200°C/400°F/gas 6.
First begin the chips by parboiling them in salted water for 3–4 minutes. Don't overcook. Drain and dry well. Put in a bowl, drizzle over the oil and toss gently but thoroughly so that each chip is coated. Arrange in one layer on a baking sheet (or 2 if necessary) and bake for 30–40 minutes or until very crisp and golden. Sprinkle with salt just before serving.

▶ To make the batter, put the flour in a bowl and whisk in enough lager to make a smooth batter. It should be approximately the thickness of double cream – the pouring kind.

▶ Dip the pieces of fish in the batter and deep-fry in hot oil until crisp and deep golden. Do not cook more than 2 pieces at a time as, if you overcrowd the pan, not only will the fish pieces stick to each other, but the temperature of the oil will drop and the batter won't crisp successfully. Use a large pan – or 2 – which should not be more than half full of oil, or use a deep-fat fryer if you have one.
Cook in batches, drain on kitchen paper and keep warm on a plate covered with kitchen paper in a low oven while you cook the rest.

▶ Serve as quickly as possible on hot plates, with more salt, the vinegar etc.

# TWICE-COOKED STILTON SOUFFLÉS

This is the perfect recipe for anyone who likes soufflés, but is afraid of trying to make one. It really is foolproof. The first stages of preparation and cooking can be done up to 24 hours in advance, then the soufflés can be effortlessly popped into the oven for their second cooking just as your guests arrive. This recipe is amazingly rich and will constitute a substantial main course if you serve it with bread and an interesting salad.

Stilton is deservedly called the king of cheeses and is a match for any European blue cheese, but you could of course use any strongly flavoured cheese you fancy.

(SERVES 6)
45 g/1½ oz butter
45 g/1½ oz flour
300 ml/10 fl oz milk
350 g/12 oz Stilton cheese,
    grated
salt and pepper
4 free-range eggs (size 3),
    separated
300 ml/10 fl oz double cream

*for the moulds*
butter
fine fresh breadcrumbs (about
    2 heaped tbsp)

▶ Preheat the oven to 200°C/400°F/gas 6.

▶ Grease 6 ramekins or small ovenproof moulds well with butter, then add breadcrumbs and swirl the mould around until all the surfaces are coated.

▶ Put the butter, flour and milk (all cold) into a saucepan and bring slowly to the boil over a low heat, stirring constantly with a wire whisk. The mixture will thicken as it comes to the boil.

▶ Turn down the heat as low as possible (use a heat diffuser if possible) and simmer for 10 minutes, stirring occasionally. This will get rid of any raw flour taste. You will have a perfectly smooth, white sauce. Remove from the heat.

▶ Stir in about two-thirds of the cheese and season the mixture with salt and pepper. Go easy on the salt as the cheese is already quite salty.

▶ Allow the mixture to cool for about 5 minutes. Lightly whisk the egg yolks and mix well into the sauce. Transfer this mixture to a large bowl. A rubber scraper will help make sure you don't leave any behind in the pan.

▶ Whisk the egg whites until stiff but not dry, and fold them into the sauce mixture.

▶ Pour into the prepared moulds and place in a bain-marie (baking tin filled with boiling water to come halfway up the moulds). Bake in the preheated oven for 20–25 minutes until risen and firm. (The soufflés are cooked to a firmer stage than traditional ones.) Leave to cool.

▶ Turn the soufflés out into greased individual gratin dishes or other individual ovenproof small dishes – or one large one (at this stage they can be kept in the fridge for up to 24 hours).

▶ If reheating from cold, preheat the oven to 220°C/425°F/gas 7. Cover the soufflés with the remaining cheese and pour the cream over, then arrange them in their dishes/dish on a baking tray and cook for about 15 minutes, until the cheese and cream are bubbling and browned around the edges. Serve immediately.

# SHEPHERD'S PIE

Shepherd's pie is traditionally made with the leftovers from a joint of lamb (hence the shepherd) whereas cottage pie is made with minced leftover roast beef. The leftover gravy would be added. This luxury version is a mixture of traditional old recipes and uses fresh minced lamb which is available from most supermarkets. The pie is good enough to serve when entertaining, particularly as the potatoes are enriched with egg yolks for a really creamy result (miss them out if calorie counting).

(SERVES 6)
2 tbsp vegetable oil
750 g/1 lb 10 oz minced lamb
25 g/1 oz butter
1 large onion, chopped
1 large clove garlic, crushed
1 tbsp plain flour
2 tbsp tomato purée
4 tbsp red wine
300 ml/10 fl oz stock (a cube is
    fine, beef, chicken or veg)
1 bay leaf
1¹/₂ tsp Worcestershire sauce
salt and pepper

*the topping*
675 g/1¹/₂ lb potatoes, peeled,
    boiled and mashed
25 g/1 oz butter
4 tbsp double cream
3 egg yolks (see above)
salt and pepper

▶ Heat the oil in a wok or frying pan and stir-fry the meat until well browned, then remove with a slotted spoon and set aside. Add the butter to the pan and stir-fry the onion over a moderate heat for about 10 minutes until soft, adding the garlic halfway through.

▶ Return the meat to the pan with the flour and tomato purée. Continue to stir-fry for 2–3 minutes. Add the wine and allow to bubble away almost completely, then add the stock, bay leaf and Worcestershire sauce and cook gently, covered, stirring occasionally, for 45 minutes. Season to taste and transfer to a suitable ovenproof dish.

▶ Meanwhile, preheat the oven to 190°C/375°F/ gas 5.

▶ Mix the potatoes with the butter, cream and egg yolks (see above), and season well with salt and pepper. Spread over the meat and make a design on top with a fork. Bake for about 20 minutes or until the potato is golden brown.

▶ Serve on warmed plates with lots of freshly cooked old-fashioned vegetables like carrots and cabbage, and some good pickles or chutney.

# COQ AU VIN

Casserole cookery has been rather out of favour until the recent appearance of Cuisine Grandmère on the menus of smart restaurants. Perhaps one of the reasons is because this kind of food is difficult to arrange elegantly on a plate. Forget elegance, bring the bubbling pot to the table, lift the lid to let out the tantalising aromas, and watch the faces of your guests.

The recipe originally was made with a cock, not a chicken, as the recipe describes. A tough old bird with lots of flavour. It is still excellent made with supermarket chicken pieces (if you insist on free-range ones), and of course doesn't take as long to cook.

Don't think you can get away with using the cheapest plonk. The cooking emphasises the flavour, not disguises it. The better the wine the better the finished dish will be!

(SERVES 6)

1 tbsp olive oil

50 g/1¾ oz butter

115 g/4 oz smoked bacon, chopped

2 onions, chopped

1 tbsp flour

6 chicken joints (cut in half to make 12 smaller pieces)

6 tbsp brandy

2 cloves garlic, finely chopped

250 g/9 oz mushrooms, sliced

3 tbsp chopped parsley

2 sprigs thyme (or ½ tsp dried)

2 bay leaves

salt and pepper

1 bottle red wine (see above)

▶ Heat the oil and butter in a deep lidded frying pan, sauté pan or wide lidded heatproof casserole, and fry the bacon and onion over a low/moderate heat for about 10 minutes or until the onions are soft and golden. Remove with a slotted spoon and transfer to a bowl. Stir the flour into the bowl and mix thoroughly.

▶ Brown the chicken all over in the fat remaining in the pan, in batches if necessary, over a medium heat. Pour over the brandy, and when hot, ignite.

▶ Return the onion mixture to the pan with the garlic, mushrooms and herbs and season well with salt and pepper. Add the wine, stir well and bring to the boil.

▶ Turn the heat as low as possible, cover the pan and simmer for 30–40 minutes or until the chicken is cooked. Transfer the chicken to a hot serving dish. If the sauce is too liquid turn up the heat and reduce to a nice saucy consistency.

▶ Serve with a simple green vegetable like beans or broccoli and for an authentic 'golden oldies' touch make hot garlic bread.

# SPAGHETTI BOLOGNESE

When the British first 'discovered' Italian food, 'Italian food' *meant* Spaghetti Bolognese, followed soon after by pizza. Spag. Bol. has since been adopted as traditional British fare and is served all over the country in pubs and greasy spoon restaurants – more often than not accompanied by chips.
Good home-made Spag. Bol. is heaven, so forget all those designer pasta dishes with squid ink, caviar and barbecued vegetables, and give Spag. Bol. another chance.
Using best-quality mince insures yours won't taste like a frozen TV dinner!

(SERVES 6)

*the sauce*

2 tbsp extra virgin olive oil

50 g/1¾ oz butter

100 g/3½ oz smoked streaky bacon, chopped

1 onion, chopped

1 carrot, chopped

1 stick celery, chopped

2 cloves garlic, very finely chopped

500 g/1 lb 2 oz lean minced beef (see above)

150 ml/5 fl oz wine (white is traditional, but red is fine)

2 tbsp tomato purée

150 ml/5 fl oz beef stock (cube is fine)

salt and pepper

4 tbsp double cream

*to serve*

450 g/1 lb spaghetti (or more according to appetite), cooked according to the instructions on the packet

freshly grated or shaved Parmesan cheese (optional)

▶ Heat the oil and butter in a heavy lidded saucepan, and stir-fry the bacon, onion, carrot and celery, stirring frequently over a medium heat for about 10 minutes or until the vegetables are softened. Add the garlic and beef and continue to cook, stirring constantly for 4–5 minutes or until the beef is well browned.

▶ Pour in the wine and allow to bubble until reduced by half. Meanwhile dissolve the tomato purée in the stock, then add this to the pan. Season well with salt and pepper, turn the heat as low as possible (use a heat-diffusing mat if possible), and cook the sauce for 2 hours uncovered. You will need to add a little water from time to time as the liquid evaporates.

▶ Just before serving, stir in the cream and check the seasoning.

▶ To serve, divide the hot cooked spaghetti between 6 heated soup dishes and spoon over the sauce. Offer Parmesan separately.

▲ Fish in Beer Batter and Chips. See page 43.

▲ No Nonsense Sherry Trifle. See page 53.

# LAMB CHOPS AND MASH

I am often asked in interviews what my favourite meal is. An impossible question as I love so many different kinds of food from Bouillabaisse to Tepanyaki. However if I really had to choose one last dish, it would be one that reminds me so much of my happy childhood. Simply cooked lamb chops and my mother's mashed potatoes – the best in the world.

My mother cooked her chops under a hot grill in a foil-lined pan until the fat was really crisp. Difficult to do if you like your lamb pink in the middle. I think crispy fat is more important than pink middle so I also cook mine quite well. A heavy iron ridged 'grill' frying pan produces excellent results.

(SERVES 6)

6 (or 12 if small) lamb chops cooked to your liking (see above)

1.5 kg/3 lb 5 oz old potatoes (I favour Maris Piper), peeled

salt and pepper

75 g/2¾ oz butter

milk

▶ This is how you make perfect mash . . . Firstly cut the potatoes into even-sized pieces. This is very important as you want them all to be perfectly cooked at the same time, otherwise you will end up with mash which still hides horrid little hard lumps.

▶ Boil in plenty of salted water until cooked. Push a knife point right in to make sure they are tender right to the centre. On the other hand don't overcook or you will end up with potato soup. Drain very thoroughly in a colander and shake out the pan to make sure it is dry. Now return the potatoes to the pan and shake over the heat for a few seconds to make sure they are really dry.

▶ Now mash quickly and thoroughly. I favour an old-fashioned masher, using an alternating, mashing and swirling whisking motion. Other modern cooks swear by a hand-held electric whisk. *On no account use a food processor or you will end up with glue.*

▶ Only when the potatoes are really thoroughly mashed and fluffy, whisk in first the butter, and then when that is melted and amalgamated, a little milk to give your preferred consistency. Season well.

▶ Serve the lamb chops and mash on hot plates with peas (no other vegetable will do in my opinion!) and perhaps some redcurrant jelly if you are feeling flash.

# STEAK AND KIDNEY PUDDING

This great British classic dish hardly needs any introduction, other than to say that if you have never made it yourself, do try – the difference between the home-made variety and the dish of the same name generally served in cafés and restaurants is immeasurable. Some recipes offer suggestions for adding things like mushrooms, or tomato purée, or a dash of Worcestershire sauce. Every cook will have their own ideas, but I give the recipe here in its simplest form which I think takes some beating.

(SERVES 6 MEDIUM OR 4 HEARTY APPETITES)

*the filling*

1 kg/2¼ lb ready-prepared steak and kidney (if buying separately allow 1 part kidney to 3 parts stewing steak – and do trim the kidneys well)

flour

salt and pepper

1 large onion, chopped

½ tsp dried mixed herbs

300 ml/10 fl oz water (or for a posher pudding, beef stock, red wine or beer – I love it made with brown ale)

*the pastry crust*

250 g/9 oz self-raising flour

125 g/4½ oz shredded suet

a good pinch salt

cold water to mix

▶ Make the pastry by mixing the flour, suet and salt in a bowl with a fork, then stirring in just enough cold water to make a firm dough. Roll out to a circle large enough to cover the bottom and sides of a 1.2 litre/2 pt pudding basin. Grease the basin. Cut out a one-third wedge from the pastry circle and reserve for the lid.

▶ Toss the meat in flour which you have seasoned well with salt and pepper. This is most successfully done in a closed plastic bag. Shake off any excess flour and put the coated meat with the onion in a large bowl. Add the herbs, season with a little more salt and pepper and mix together well.

▶ Form the bigger bit of pastry into a loose cone over your hand and ease it into the prepared basin, overlapping the cut edges and sealing with a little water. Dampen the top edge of the pastry.

▶ Fill the bowl almost to the top with the meat mixture. Although the pastry will expand, the meat will shrink in cooking so you don't have to allow any extra space for this. Pour in the water (or other liquid of your choice). It should not quite cover the contents.

▶ Roll out the remaining third of pastry to a circle which will fit the top of the bowl. Fit this on top of the filling and press the edges together to seal.

▶ Cover the top of the pudding very tightly with

oiled kitchen foil, folding a pleat into it before you start to allow for expansion. Secure with string.

▶ Stand the basin in a suitable saucepan (a long strip of foil laid under the base of the bowl and up the sides will make it easier to remove the hot pudding from the pan when it is cooked), and pour boiling water into the pan to come two-thirds of the way up the bowl. Put a lid on the pan and cook over a low heat so that the water is just simmering for 4 hours. Check the water level every so often for evaporation and top up with more boiling water. (The whole thing can be cooked in a fraction of the time in a microwave. Follow the instruction manual.)

▶ Steak and kidney pudding is traditionally brought to the table in the bowl that it was cooked in. This should be wrapped in a clean tea towel or napkin. Serve with whatever fresh vegetables you like (carrots, I feel are almost obligatory), and offer a choice of English mustard and horseradish sauce.

# Steak and Kidney Pie

Use the same ingredients and quantities as for the Steak and Kidney Pudding filling above, but place in a heavy saucepan and simmer over a very low heat (use a heat diffuser if possible), tightly covered, for about 2 hours, or until the meat is tender. Alternatively cook in a covered ovenproof casserole in a low oven (160°C/325°F/gas 3) for the same time. Allow to cool then tip into a suitable deep pie dish.

(SERVES 4–6)

▶ Preheat the oven to 200°C/400°F/gas 6.

▶ Make a suet pastry as above, but using only 175 g/6 oz self-raising flour and 85 g/3 oz suet. Roll out and cover the filling, dampening the edges of the dish to make the pastry stick. Use a pie funnel or an up-turned egg cup if necessary to keep the crust raised in the middle. Use the pastry trimmings to cut out decorative leaves or other shapes for the top of the pie if liked. Brush the pastry with a glaze made from an egg yolk mixed with a little milk and bake for about 30 minutes, or until the crust is crisp and golden.

▶ Serve with the same accompaniments as for Steak and Kidney Pudding.

# GRATIN DAUPHINOISE

I love potatoes in all guises but this I think is the Rolls Royce of potato recipes. If you are on a diet, however, ignore this recipe and eat a baked potato instead – low-cal. versions simply don't work.

This is one of those classic dishes with as many 'authentic' recipes as there are cooks who make it. This is my version and it works very well. Many recipes contain no cheese, but I love it with, as it makes a meal in itself if accompanied by a good salad and some crusty warm bread.

I slice my potatoes in my food processor which performs the task in seconds. It is important not to wash the potatoes after slicing as this would remove the starch that gives the finished dish its creamy homogeneous texture.

(SERVES 6)

1.5 kg/3 lb 5 oz large waxy
   potatoes, peeled and cut
   into very thin slices
300 ml/10 fl oz single cream
150 ml/5 fl oz milk
25 g/1 oz butter
1 clove garlic, crushed
150 g/5$^{1}/_{2}$ oz Gruyère cheese,
   grated
salt and pepper
freshly grated nutmeg

▶ Preheat the oven to 190°C/375°F/gas 5.
Put the potatoes, cream and milk in a large saucepan and bring to the boil. Turn down the heat immediately and simmer over the lowest possible heat, stirring constantly for about 5 minutes, being very careful not to let it burn.

▶ Meanwhile use the butter to grease a shallow ovenproof dish and then spread the crushed garlic over the bottom of the dish. Using a slotted spoon, remove the potatoes from the pan and layer them in the dish with the grated cheese (remembering to leave a bit over for the top), seasoning each layer with salt, pepper and nutmeg.

▶ Pour over the creamy liquid from the pan and sprinkle over the remaining cheese. Bake for 1$^1/_2$ hours or until the potatoes are quite tender and the top golden brown.

# NO NONSENSE SHERRY TRIFLE

My mother's recipe – the best – never fails to win compliments. I have tried going to all the trouble of making the custard with eggs, and I can honestly say this version made with everyday custard powder (I use Bird's) tastes best. Sherry trifle traditionally should be made and served from a cut-glass bowl – if you have one!

(SERVES 6 GENEROUSLY)
225 g/8 oz trifle sponges
150 g/5½ oz best-quality
   raspberry jam
150 ml/5 fl oz dry or medium
   sherry
850 ml/1½ pt custard (made
   according to the
   instructions on the packet),
   cooled slightly
300 ml/10 fl oz double cream,
   whipped until stiff
flaked almonds to decorate

▶ Slice each sponge cake in half across and spread thickly with jam. Arrange jam side up in the bottom of a glass bowl and pour over the sherry.

▶ Pour over the slightly cooled custard, prodding the sponges a little with a fork to ensure that the custard seeps down through every space to the bottom of the bowl. Chill until set.

▶ Cover with whipped cream and garnish with almonds.

# STEAMED TREACLE SPONGE WITH BUTTERSCOTCH CUSTARD

There is no pudding in the world to touch a real English steamed pudding. This is perhaps the ultimate.

(SERVES 6–8)

115 g/4 oz unsalted butter

55 g/2 oz soft brown sugar

2 large eggs (size 1)

225 g/8 oz self-raising flour, sifted

1/4 tsp ground ginger

grated rind of 1 1/2 lemons (preferably unwaxed)

approx. 75–85 ml/2 1/2–3 fl oz warmed milk

2 tbsp treacle

2 tbsp golden syrup

▶ Cream the butter and the sugar until pale. Add the eggs, sifted flour, ginger and grated lemon rind. Mix well. Slowly add the milk until you have a dropping consistency. (I do all this in a food processor.)

▶ Warm the treacle and syrup and pour into a buttered 15 cm/6 in pudding basin. Spoon the sponge mixture on top and cover the basin tightly with buttered pleated foil. Secure with string.

▶ Put the basin in a large pan and pour in boiling water to come halfway up the basin. Cover the pan and allow the pudding to steam for 1 1/2 hours, checking the water level occasionally and topping up if it has boiled away. (This pudding will cook in about 5 minutes in a microwave on 100% power – replace the foil with microwave film.)

▶ To serve, turn out immediately, slice, and pour over the following sauce.

# BUTTERSCOTCH CUSTARD

(SERVES 6–8)

1 vanilla pod

1 x 100 g tin condensed milk

300 ml/10 fl oz double cream

4 egg yolks

25 g/1 oz soft dark brown sugar

1 tsp cornflour, mixed with a drop of milk

▶ Split the vanilla pod and place in a small saucepan with the condensed milk and double cream. Bring to the boil, take off the heat and allow to cool. Remove and discard the vanilla pod.

▶ In a small saucepan, cream the yolks and sugar, then gradually whisk in the flavoured cream, then the cornflour and milk. Over a very low heat bring the custard to not quite boiling point, whisking constantly, until thickened. Do not allow it to boil.

# Chapter 4

# TV DINNERS

Although I would be the first to extol the undoubted virtues of sitting around a table to eat and enjoy food properly, I can hardly preach what I don't practise, and much as I like the idea of sitting down to a candle-lit supper with a nicely laundered linen napkin every evening, the reality is very different. I do actually cook a proper meal from scratch every evening (well, it is my job, and I am usually testing a new recipe), but, like so many other people at the end of a busy day, my partner and I sit and eat from trays on knees in front of the tele.

Shocking, I know, but I thought I had better get it off my chest before the tabloid press makes a big scandal out of it. ('TV chef in food horror scandal'?)

So here is a great selection of recipes from substantial sandwiches to slow-cooked casseroles, which take up the minimum of mid-week time or effort, and definitely taste best when eaten in front of *EastEnders*, *The Bill* or *Ab. Fab.* repeats.

*PS I have tried eating them whilst sitting up properly at a table (e.g. when snooker or sheepdog trials are the most interesting choice on the box), and they still taste surprisingly good!*

# SIRLOIN STEAK IN CIABATTA WITH CARAMELISED SHALLOTS

What can I say? Add a glass of good red wine and the Eurovision song contest . . . !

(MAKES 2 SANDWICHES)
2 thin sirloin steaks weighing approx. 125 g/4¹/₂ oz each
salt and pepper
1 ciabatta loaf, cut in half widthways, heated in a medium oven until crisp
French mustard

*the shallots*
25 g/1 oz butter
250 g/9 oz shallots, peeled (a few seconds in boiling water makes this much easier)
1 heaped tsp sugar
salt and pepper

*to serve*
salad (whatever takes your fancy, optional)

▶ First cook the shallots. Melt the butter in a small saucepan. Add the prepared shallots. Sprinkle over the sugar, season with salt and pepper and pour over enough cold water to just cover the shallots. Bring to the boil and cook over a low–medium heat, stirring occasionally, until all the liquid has evaporated and the shallots are covered with a sticky golden glaze.

▶ Trim any excess fat off the steaks, then season well on both sides with salt and pepper. Then either grill, or fry in a lightly oiled (preferably non-stick) frying pan, or a heavy iron ridged 'grill' frying pan for a couple of minutes on each side or until cooked to your liking.

▶ Spread the bread slices liberally with the mustard, then make into sandwiches with the hot steaks and shallots.

▶ Serve immediately (with optional knives and forks), garnishing the plates with salad if liked.

# CROQUE MONSIEUR

 There are, as with all classic recipes, endless variations on this French hot sandwich. Some versions involve a sort of thick béchamel sauce as well as the ham and cheese filling. The worst kind are prepared in advance and heated through in a microwave, which melts the cheese well but turns the bread into a damp soggy mess. This is the simplest version and, I think, the best way of making a good Croque Monsieur.

(MAKES 2)
4 slices white bread (ready
    sliced is fine)
butter
approx. 100 g/3¹/₂ oz Gruyère
    or Emmental cheese, grated
approx. 75 g/2³/₄ oz cooked
    ham (preferably sliced from
    the bone)

to serve
Dijon mustard

▶ Butter the slices of bread generously on one side, then make neat sandwiches with a cheese, ham, cheese layer between the bread slices which must be *buttered side out*.

▶ Heat a dry (preferably non-stick) frying pan over a low-medium heat and fry the sandwiches for 1–2 minutes on each side or until the bread is golden and crisp and the cheese has melted. (You could also use an electric sandwich toaster.)

▶ Serve immediately with Dijon mustard on the side and a knife and fork.

# HOT CROISSANTS STUFFED WITH SMOKED SALMON

 New Yorkers love bagels filled with lox (smoked salmon) and cream cheese. Using warmed croissants turns this brilliant combination of flavours into a 'proper hot meal', particularly if you add a nice bit of healthy salad to counteract the richness.

(SERVES 2)
2 croissants, heated
125 g/4¹/₂ oz smoked salmon
2 tbsp fromage frais or
    Greek-style yogurt
pepper
fresh dill (optional)
pickled cocktail gherkins

▶ Split each warm croissant in half, then fill with smoked salmon. Add fromage frais or yogurt, a twist of pepper and a sprig of dill (if used).

▶ Serve immediately on warmed plates with a little pile of gherkins.

# BREAKFAST ON SALAD

This trendy warm salad is a great way of enjoying all the flavours of breakfast as a main course at any time of the day. You can of course vary the ingredients, adding and subtracting to include your favourite combination. Mine would definitely include a few slices of crispy fried black pudding! If you are trying to cut back on fat, omit the croûtons or make them from toasted bread and substitute a poached egg for the fried one and let the runny yolk act as the 'dressing'.

(SERVES 2)

2 handfuls of your favourite salad leaves

6–8 crisply fried or grilled bacon rashers (I would choose smoked streaky)

6–8 cherry tomatoes, halved and grilled until bubbling

2 free-range eggs, fried (keep the yolks runny) in a little olive oil (see above)

2 tbsp white wine vinegar

salt and pepper

*the croûtons*

2 slices of bread, fried crisp in bacon fat or olive oil and cut into little squares (see above)

▶ Have the salad leaves ready in little mounds on 2 large plates and pile on the bacon, tomatoes and eggs.

▶ Stir the vinegar into the remaining oil in the pan you cooked the eggs in to make a little warm dressing. Season it with salt and pepper, and pour over the salad.

▶ To serve, scatter over the croûtons and eat at once.

# Mediterranean Salad

This colourful salad makes a great light meal for 4 if served with lots of interesting bread, but would also serve 6 as the first course of a 'proper' meal. I like to serve a really good extra virgin olive oil, lemon wedges and coarse salt and pepper, so that everyone can dress their salad to their own liking as the Italians do, rather than making a vinaigrette.

(SERVES 4 AS A LIGHT MAIN COURSE
OR 6 AS A STARTER)
125 g/4$\frac{1}{2}$ oz green beans
350 g/12 oz baby new potatoes
1 bulb fennel
1 head chicory
$\frac{1}{2}$ bunch small spring onions
4 hard-boiled free-range eggs
4 tomatoes
125 g/4$\frac{1}{2}$ oz olives (whatever
    kind/kinds you fancy)
1 x 55 g tin anchovies, drained
    and chopped (optional)

to serve
good extra virgin olive oil
lemon wedges
black pepper
coarse salt (I like Maldon)

▶ Cook the beans and potatoes separately until just tender. Drain well and cool.

▶ Thinly slice the fennel, and separate the chicory leaves. Trim the spring onions, and halve larger ones lengthways.

▶ Quarter the hard-boiled eggs, and cut the tomatoes into wedges.

▶ Combine all the salad ingredients in an attractive serving bowl. Serve at room temperature and offer the dressing ingredients separately.

# VIETNAMESE CHICKEN SALAD

In the distinctively delicious cuisine of Vietnam, the classic combination of fresh mint and coriander, chillies, lime juice and oriental fish sauce can become quite addictive. Try my version of a Vietnamese dish and see for yourself.

Don't be put off by the seemingly long list of ingredients, they are all available from large supermarkets, and once assembled the dish takes only minutes to prepare. (If serving this as a main course, allow the equivalent of 1 chicken breast per serving.) Oriental fish sauce is available from oriental shops and large supermarkets. There is no real substitute, but light soy sauce mixed with a mashed anchovy or two will do at a pinch.)

If you are cooking the chicken specially for this recipe it will taste even better if 'grilled' in a heavy ridged iron frying pan or, best of all, barbecued.

(SERVES **6** AS A FIRST COURSE)

*the salad*

**500 g/1 lb 2 oz shredded or sliced cooked chicken**

**500 g/1 lb 2 oz finely shredded white, red or green cabbage**

**150 g/5¹/₂ oz carrot**

**6 spring onions**

**3 tbsp each of coarsely chopped mint and coriander leaves**

*the dressing*

**3 tbsp fresh lime juice**

**3 tbsp oriental fish sauce**

**1 tbsp white wine vinegar**

**2 cloves garlic, crushed**

**2 tbsp sugar**

**3 tbsp vegetable oil**

**2 chillies, deseeded and chopped**

*to garnish*

**50 g/1³/₄ oz dry roasted peanuts, chopped**

**small mint and coriander sprigs**

**prawn crackers (optional but very good)**

▶ Put the chicken and cabbage into a bowl.

▶ Cut the carrot into julienne strips or long thin slivers with a swivel-bladed vegetable peeler. Cut the spring onions into long thin strips (including the good green parts).

▶ Add the carrot and spring onion to the chicken and cabbage, along with the herbs.

▶ Now make the dressing. Put the first 5 ingredients in a large bowl and whisk to try and dissolve the sugar as much as possible, then whisk in the oil and chopped chillies. Leave for about 30 minutes for the flavours to develop, then mix in the salad ingredients gently but thoroughly.

▶ To serve, divide between 6 plates or bowls, sprinkle with chopped peanuts, garnish with mint and coriander sprigs, and serve with prawn crackers if liked.

# OVEN-FRIED CHICKEN AND WEDGIES WITH SOURED CREAM

 This is based on an American recipe, but don't be put off by the thought of fast food chains, the home-made variety is infinitely better and tastes of chicken, rather than merely of overly flavoured coatings. This method 'fries' the chicken in the oven, which is much less trouble, mess and smell. I can't pretend that this is exactly a low-calorie treat, but everyone needs to have a little fried food occasionally – it's good for the soul!

(SERVES 6)

125ml/4 fl oz vegetable oil

115 g/4 oz butter

3 cloves garlic, sliced

175 g/6 oz flour

1 heaped tsp salt

2 tsp black pepper

2 tsp paprika

2 heaped tsp dried marjoram

12 small chicken pieces
(drumsticks, thighs,
wings etc.)

to serve

oven-fried potato wedgies (see
page 43)

soured cream or crème fraîche

simple green salad

▶ Preheat the oven to 200°C/400°F/gas 6.

▶ Put the oil, butter and garlic in the roasting tin and then into the oven for about 10 minutes, or until the butter has melted and the garlic has turned golden. Do not allow the garlic to become too dark. Remove from the oven, remove the garlic with a slotted spoon and discard. Allow the oil/butter mixture to cool for 10 minutes.

▶ Put the flour and seasonings into a large plastic bag, close tightly and shake to mix thoroughly.

▶ Working with 2–3 pieces of chicken at a time, roll them first in the garlic-flavoured oil/butter mixture, allowing any excess to drip off back into the pan, then drop them into the bag of seasoned flour. Close tightly and shake to coat well. Remove the coated pieces from the bag, shaking off any excess flour, and arrange them on a large plate or a piece of foil or greaseproof paper while you coat the rest.

▶ Return the chicken pieces to the pan (which will still contain some of the oil/butter mixture), skin side down and bake for 45 minutes, basting after 30. Turn the pieces over and bake for another 10–15 minutes or until crisp and brown.

▶ Serve with hot potato wedgies, soured cream or crème fraîche and a simple green salad.

# LAZY CHICKEN 'N' RICE

Based on a recipe from the Caribbean, this is a wonderfully tasty main-course dish which 'cooks itself' so that the finished dish contains crispy skinned chicken sitting on a bed of spicy moist rice with vegetables. The quantity of uncooked rice will seem very little, but it swells enormously during cooking. I invented this recipe five years ago as something easy and inexpensive to feed hungry students. I can honestly say that this is my favourite recipe ever, as it is ridiculously easy, can be varied endlessly (I have done it with lamb chops, sausages and all kinds of flavourings) so long as you stick to the proportions of rice and liquid – and it always tastes totally fab.

(SERVES 6)

6 chicken portions

salt and pepper

3 tbsp corn or sunflower oil

1 small onion, chopped

250 g/9 oz mushrooms, sliced

250 g/9 oz basmati or other
    long-grain rice, rinsed and
    dried

850 ml/1½ pt boiling chicken
    stock (a cube is fine)

4 tbsp lime (substitute lemon if
    you can't find lime) juice

3 cloves garlic, crushed

3 sprigs thyme (or 1 level tsp
    dried)

1 heaped tsp chilli powder (or
    more to taste)

▶ Preheat the oven to 200°C/400°F/gas 6.
Season the chicken pieces with pepper and salt. Heat the oil in a large frying pan (preferably non-stick) and fry the chicken pieces over a low/medium heat for about 5 minutes on each side or until lightly browned. (Work in manageable batches if your pan is small.)

▶ Meanwhile grease a shallow ovenproof dish and scatter the chopped onion, the sliced mushrooms and rice over the bottom. On top of this, arrange the chicken pieces in 1 layer, skin side up.

▶ In a jug or bowl combine the stock, lime juice, garlic, thyme and chilli powder and pour this over the chicken and vegetables. Place in the oven uncovered and leave to cook, undisturbed, for about 1 hour or until the chicken is cooked and all the stock has been absorbed by the rice.

▶ Serve with a simple green vegetable like beans, or with a salad.

# Extra Special Fried Rice

Traditionally Chinese 'special fried rice' is served as an accompaniment to several other dishes. Here the garnishes which make the fried rice 'special' are increased in size and quantity so that it becomes a satisfying meal in itself. Although you can make this with leftover cooked rice it is very much better if made with freshly cooked rice.

(SERVES **6** AS A MAIN DISH)

3 tbsp vegetable oil

1 x 2.5 cm/1 in cube fresh ginger, finely chopped

4 rashers lean smoked bacon, chopped

2 onions, chopped

2 cloves garlic, finely chopped

1 red pepper, deseeded and cut into 1 cm/$\frac{1}{2}$ in squares, diamonds, or any shape you fancy

225 g/8 oz drained tinned straw mushrooms (1 large can)

150 g/5$\frac{1}{2}$ oz frozen peas

200 g/7 oz cooked chicken, shredded

200 g/7 oz cooked and peeled large prawns

350 g/12 oz basmati rice, cooked and drained

salt

*the omelette*

3 eggs, lightly beaten

1 tbsp soy sauce

2 spring onions, finely chopped

vegetable oil for frying

*to garnish*

6 large prawns in their shells (optional)

▶ First make the omelette. Mix the eggs with the soy sauce and chopped spring onion then, using a very little oil in a preferably non-stick frying pan, make two thin omelettes using half the mixture each time. Roll the omelettes up and cut across at 1 cm/$\frac{1}{2}$ in intervals to produce long noodle-like strips. Reserve.

▶ Heat the oil in a wok or large deep-sided frying or sauté pan and stir-fry the ginger and bacon over a moderate heat for 1 minute. Add the onion and garlic and continue to stir-fry for another minute. Add the pepper, mushrooms, peas and chicken and stir-fry for 30 seconds, then add the prawns and cooked rice, season with salt and stir-fry for 45 seconds.

▶ Divide between 6 plates or bowls, arrange the omelette strips on top, garnish with the whole prawns (if used) and serve immediately.

# SPAGHETTI WITH MEATBALLS

These meatballs are particularly good as they are flavoured with Parmesan. (It's worth making double quantities and freezing half for another day.) The unusual creamy sauce makes them especially delicious.

(SERVES 6 AS A FIRST COURSE OR 4 AS A MAIN COURSE)

450 g/1 lb spaghetti, cooked according to the instructions on the packet

250 g/9 oz extra lean minced beef

125 g/4$\frac{1}{2}$ oz minced chicken or turkey

50 g/1$\frac{3}{4}$ oz smoked streaky bacon, finely chopped

25 g/1 oz fresh white breadcrumbs

45 g/1$\frac{1}{2}$ oz Parmesan cheese, freshly grated

1 egg

salt and pepper

a pinch ground nutmeg

olive oil for frying

450 ml/16 fl oz single cream

1 heaped tbsp tomato purée

*to serve*

3 ripe tomatoes, chopped

▶ Thoroughly combine the minced meats, chopped bacon, breadcrumbs, Parmesan and egg, and season with salt, pepper and nutmeg. Go steady on the salt as the Parmesan is quite salty. If the mixture is too sticky, add a few more breadcrumbs.

▶ Form the mixture into small balls, about 2 cm/ $\frac{3}{4}$ in across.

▶ Lightly oil a preferably non-stick frying pan and stir-fry the meatballs for about 5 minutes over a low heat until they are browned all over.

▶ Pour off all but the merest film of fat from the pan and add the cream and tomato purée. Season with salt and pepper and simmer very gently for another 10 minutes. The meatballs will soften and the sauce will thicken.

▶ To serve, divide the cooked and drained pasta between 6 heated dishes, pour over the meatballs and sauce, and top with the chopped tomato.

▲ Sirloin Steak in Ciabatta with Caramelised Shallots. See page 56.

▲ Vietnamese Chicken Salad. See page 60.

▲ Rack of Lamb with Roast Aubergine, Chick Pea and Rocket. See page 79.

▲ Helter-skelter Duck and Filo Parcels. See page 83.

# SWEETCORN, ONION AND STILTON TART

The filling for this tasty tart is lighter and less expensive than a traditional quiche filling. Good hot, warm or cold it will serve 4 people for a light meal if accompanied by a salad, but will stretch to 6 for a main meal if served with potatoes and lots of vegetables.

You could of course use any kind of strongly flavoured cheese for this recipe but somehow the sharp saltiness of the Stilton is a perfect foil for the sweetness of the sweetcorn.

(SERVES 4–6)

250 g/9 oz shortcrust pastry
  (see page 19)
25 g/1 oz butter
2 medium onions, chopped
1 tsp dry English mustard
1 rounded tbsp flour
300 ml/10 fl oz milk
75 g/2¾ oz Stilton cheese (see
  above), crumbled
1 egg, lightly beaten
125 g/4½ oz sweetcorn
  (thawed if frozen, drained if
  tinned)
salt and pepper

▶ Preheat the oven to 200°C/400°F/gas 6.

▶ Roll out the pastry and line a 23 cm/9 in loose-bottomed deep-sided flan tin. Chill while you make the filling.

▶ Melt the butter in a saucepan and cook the onion for 5–10 minutes over a medium heat, stirring constantly until soft and golden. Add the mustard and flour, mix well then add the milk and bring to the boil, stirring constantly. Turn down the heat and simmer for 2–3 minutes.

▶ Add the cheese, then remove from the heat and allow to cool for 2–3 minutes. Stir in the egg and sweetcorn and season with salt and pepper. Pour into the pastry case. Bake for 30–40 minutes or until the filling is set and the top golden.

▶ Serve with potatoes (baked are good with this) and fresh seasonal vegetables.

# CUMBERLAND PIE

Quick and easy to cook and bring together, this savoury pie-with-a-difference makes a hearty mealtime treat.
Good hot, warm or cold it will serve 4 people for a light meal if accompanied by a salad, but will stretch to 6 for a main meal if served with your favourite chutney and lots of fresh vegetables.

(SERVES 4–6)

450 g/1 lb Cumberland sausages (if you can find the sort sold in one continuous coil, even better!)

1 tbsp vegetable oil

1 large onion, finely chopped

1 x 85 g packet sage and onion stuffing mix, made up according to the instructions on the packet

350 g/12 oz shortcrust pastry (see page 19), or thawed if frozen

1 egg yolk, mixed with a little milk, to glaze (optional)

▶ Preheat the oven to 200°C/400°F/gas 6.
Grill the sausages until done but not too browned. (If you are using the continuous link sort, keep it in one piece and cook it in a spiral shape, securing with a wooden cocktail stick.) Leave to cool. Remove stick.

▶ Heat the oil in a frying pan and stir-fry the onion for about 10 minutes or until soft and then mix thoroughly into the stuffing mix. Leave to cool.

▶ Roll out half the pastry and use to line a 20 cm/ 8 in pie tin. Arrange the sausages (sausage) in a spiral in the pastry case, then cover with the stuffing mix, poking it well down into the gaps.

▶ Roll out the remaining pastry to make a lid. Dampen the edges to seal. Decorate with the pastry scraps, and brush with egg glaze (if used). Bake in the preheated oven for 30–40 minutes or until golden brown.

▶ Serve hot or cold.

# COWBOY SAUSAGE AND BEAN POT

Sausage and beans are successful partners in cuisines all over the world – the Cassoulet of the South-West of France being perhaps the most famous dish. This is my version of a much simpler one-pot dish from the USA. Although the cooking time in this recipe is quite long, it is very quick and simple once you have assembled the ingredients. Perfect to cook on Sunday evening and keep in the fridge ready for a comforting hearty meal during the week.

(SERVES 6)

500 g/1 lb 2 oz dried butter beans

3 sticks celery, chopped

2 onions, chopped

1 green pepper, deseeded, trimmed and chopped

125 g/4½ oz smoked streaky bacon, chopped

3 cloves garlic, crushed

1 tbsp black treacle

1 tsp mixed herbs

½ tsp cumin seeds

salt and pepper

1 rounded tsp chilli powder (or more to taste)

6 meaty pork sausages (Toulouse or Italian style would be ideal)

600 ml/1 pt bitter (beer)

▶ Soak the beans in cold water overnight, then drain. Transfer to a large saucepan, cover with 2.25 litres/4 pt cold water, bring to the boil and simmer for 1 hour or until tender. Drain and mix in a large bowl with all the other ingredients except the sausages and beer.

▶ Meanwhile, preheat the oven to 180°C/350°F/ gas 4.

▶ Spread half the bean mixture in the bottom of a large lidded casserole, lay the sausages on top and cover with the remaining bean mixture.

▶ Pour over the beer, cover tightly and cook for 3 hours. If there is still quite a lot of liquid left, remove the lid for the last half hour.

▶ Serve hot with a green vegetable or salad.

# STIR-FRY BEEF WITH PEPPERS AND WALNUTS

Where would we all be without our woks? The 'stir-fry' is perhaps the ultimate in 'fast fab food', as it is almost instant, provides masses of flavour and is easy to eat on your knees – even with chopsticks.

I would serve this with plain boiled rice and simply boiled or steamed greens (oriental ones if your supermarket has them) drizzled with Chinese oyster sauce.

**(SERVES 6)**

750 g/1 lb 10 oz sirloin or rump
    steak
4 tbsp soy sauce
3 cloves garlic, crushed
2 tsp cornflour
1 heaped tsp sugar
4 tbsp vegetable oil
3 peppers (any colours, mixed
    is nice), deseeded and cut
    into bite-sized pieces
175 g/6 oz walnut pieces
5 cm/2 in cube fresh ginger,
    thinly sliced

▶ Cut the steak into thin bite-sized slices and reserve.

▶ Combine the soy sauce, garlic, cornflour and sugar in a bowl and then add the beef strips and mix well until each piece is coated. Set aside for 20–30 minutes to marinate.

▶ Heat the oil in a wok or frying pan and add the meat mixture. Stir-fry for 2–3 minutes, then add the pepper, nuts and ginger and continue to stir-fry for 3–4 minutes more.

▶ Serve immediately.

# VEGETABLE AND CASHEW NUT BIRYANI

A simplified version of a classic Indian dish, this is much less work than the 'authentic' versions but nevertheless delicious. Served with rice and pickles and perhaps a bowl of thick yogurt flavoured with garlic and a simple cucumber salad, this makes a very satisfying one-pot meal for vegetarians and carnivores alike.

(SERVES 6)

1 tbsp vegetable oil

50 g/1¾ oz butter

1 onion, chopped

2 cloves garlic, finely chopped

250 g/9 oz diced carrot

250 g/9 oz sliced green beans

250 g/9 oz roughly chopped green pepper

150 g/5½ oz unsalted cashew nuts

1 tbsp curry powder (your favourite Indian one) or more to taste

1 heaped tsp dark brown sugar

1 level tsp salt

150 ml/5 fl oz Greek-style yogurt

¼ tsp saffron steeped in 2 tbsp warm water (optional but authentic and very good)

300 g/10½ oz basmati rice, cooked and drained

3 heaped tbsp chopped coriander

▶ Preheat the oven to 200°C/400°F/gas 6.

▶ Heat the oil and butter in a wok or large frying pan and stir-fry the onion over a moderate heat for about 10 minutes or until soft, adding the garlic halfway through.

▶ Add the vegetables and half the nuts, with the curry powder, sugar and salt, and continue to stir-fry for another 3–4 minutes until beginning to soften. Remove from the heat.

▶ Mix the yogurt with the saffron infusion and stir into the vegetable mixture with the rice and half the coriander.

▶ Transfer to a lightly oiled ovenproof dish, sprinkle with the remaining nuts, cover with a lid or foil and bake for about 30 minutes or until piping hot.

▶ Scatter with the remaining coriander and serve at once.

# HONEY CHILLI PRAWNS ON NOODLES

I adore anything served with oriental egg noodles. Sharwoods make excellent ones which are available in most supermarkets. Two packets will feed 6 people – simply cook them according to the instructions on the packet.

(SERVES 6)

2 tbsp vegetable oil

2 cloves garlic, chopped

1 x 2.5 cm/1 in cube fresh
    ginger, grated

1–2 red or green chillies,
    deseeded and chopped (or
    more to taste)

750 g/1 lb 10 oz shelled raw
    prawns (thawed if frozen)

1 bunch spring onions, sliced
    diagonally (include good
    green parts)

2 tbsp runny honey

juice of 1 lemon

1 tbsp soy sauce


to serve

cooked noodles (see above)

chopped fresh coriander
    (optional)

▶ Heat the oil in a wok (or large frying pan) and stir-fry the garlic, ginger and chilli over a high heat for 1 minute.

▶ Add the prawns and spring onions and stir-fry for 1–2 minutes or just until the prawns turn pink. Do not overcook or the prawns will become rubbery.

▶ Add the honey, lemon juice and soy sauce and allow to bubble up.

▶ Serve immediately over the drained noodles and sprinkle with fresh coriander if you love it as I do.

# FISH CHOWDER

Based on an old American recipe, this one-dish meal is a cross between a soup and a stew. It takes only minutes to make and will soothe and sustain, without overly challenging the taste buds.

Use any firm fish you like – a mixture is excellent, particularly if you include some smoked fish. I like to use approximately equal quantities of cod, salmon and smoked haddock.

(SERVES 6)

1 tbsp vegetable oil
150 g/5¹/₂ oz smoked streaky bacon, sliced across into 1 cm/¹/₂ in pieces
2 onions, chopped
1 red pepper, deseeded and cut into 1 cm/¹/₂ in pieces
500 g/1 lb 2 oz potatoes (Jerseys would be heaven), scrubbed and cut into ¹/₂ in/ 1 cm dice
1 heaped tbsp cornflour
1.2 litres/2 pt full-fat milk
500 g/1 lb 2 oz skinned fish fillets (see above), cut into bite-sized pieces
25 g/1 oz sweetcorn (thawed if frozen, drained if tinned)
salt and pepper
100 g/3¹/₂ oz cooked shelled prawns (thawed if frozen)
dash Worcestershire sauce

to garnish
25 g/1 oz butter, diced
chopped dill, chervil, fennel or parsley

▶ Heat the oil in a heavy-bottomed saucepan and fry the bacon pieces over a low heat, or until they render their fat. Turn up the heat and fry until crisp, turning as necessary. Remove the cooked bacon with a slotted spoon and set aside.

▶ Stir-fry the onion and pepper in the remaining fat for about 5 minutes or until the onion is softened but not browned. Add the potatoes, and stir-fry for 1 minute. Return half the bacon to the pan, but reserve the remainder for garnish.

▶ Dissolve the cornflour in a little of the milk. Adding the remaining milk to the potato mixture, then stir the cornflour mixture into this. Bring to the boil and simmer, over the lowest possible heat, stirring occasionally for about 10–15 minutes or until the potatoes are completely tender.

▶ Add the fish pieces and sweetcorn kernels to the pan and season well with salt and pepper. Continue to simmer for 2–3 minutes or until the fish is just cooked. Add the prawns (the soup will heat them through sufficiently without further cooking) and Worcestershire sauce to taste. Check the seasoning.

▶ Serve in heated bowls and sprinkle with the butter pieces, the reserved crisped bacon and chopped herbs if liked.

# BARBECUED SPARE RIBS

Barbecued meat in America meant and still often does mean that the meat is cooked over charcoal and served with a spicy sweet and sour sauce. Nowadays, however, particularly in home cooking, the meat is often either cooked under a domestic grill or in the oven and either basted with or cooked in one of the countless variations of the ever-popular barbecue sauce.

A nice big leafy salad, eaten American-style as a first course, turns this into an easy but well balanced meal.

(SERVES 6, 4–5 RIBS EACH)
1.5kg/3 lb 5 oz 'American style' pork spare ribs

*the sauce*
1 tbsp vegetable oil
½ onion, finely chopped
1 clove garlic, crushed
6 tbsp tomato ketchup
2 tsp dry English mustard
3 tbsp Worcestershire sauce
2 tbsp vinegar
3 tbsp maple syrup (large supermarkets)
½–1 tsp Tabasco sauce (or more to taste)
salt and pepper
5 tbsp water

*to serve*
plainly cooked white rice

▶ Preheat the oven to 220°C/425°F/gas 7.

▶ Arrange the spare ribs in 1 large or 2 medium roasting pans, cover with foil, and cook for 15 minutes. Remove the foil and pour off and discard any fat and watery juices. Reduce the oven temperature to 180°C/350°F/gas 4.

▶ Meanwhile heat the oil in a saucepan and cook the onion over a medium heat, stirring occasionally for 5–10 minutes or until softened but not coloured. Add the rest of the ingredients, bring to the boil, turn down the heat and simmer for 2–3 minutes.

▶ Pour the sauce over the ribs in the pan, tossing to coat well, then bake uncovered for 1 hour, basting every 10–15 minutes. (Swap the pans around top to bottom in the oven halfway through if using two pans.)

▶ Serve immediately on plainly cooked white rice with any remaining sauce dribbled over. Do provide plenty of napkins, or, even better, wet flannels as the only way to enjoy these ribs is by eating them in your fingers.

# CHAPTER 5

# A LITTLE BIT OF OOH LA LA

I always try and correct people when they introduce me as a chef, because I am not. The title 'chef' infers that its bearer has attended a professional course at college or at least served a lengthy and arduous apprenticeship in professional kitchens. Chefs cook food which people pay for. It also entitles them to wear 'chef's whites'.

Having had no professional training (well, only a week's prize at a cookery school in Paris learning how to make pastry), I am decidedly a domestic cook, and describe myself as a professional amateur (it also means that on TV I don't have to wear the same old boring white outfit day in and day out).

Someone recently insisted, however, that although I might not be professionally trained, I couldn't dispute the fact that I was a 'TV chef'. I have almost given in to this honorary title after I was recently invited to 'guest' for a week in the very-posh-indeed Four Seasons Hotel overlooking Hyde Park in London. I was invited to create a different main-course dish for each day of the week. The recipes were designed to fit in with the elegant style of the restaurant, but because I am so used to creating recipes which are quick and easy to prepare (even for a 'proper' dinner party I don't want to spend hours in the kitchen when I could be out shopping), they are still well within the capabilities of even the most modest cook.

I have included the recipes for even decidedly chef-y dishes here, along with another three favourites which should delight and impress your friends so much that they might give *you* the honorary title of 'chef' . . .

# SPICED DUCK BREAST WITH SHALLOT, BRAMBLE COMPOTE AND SWEET POTATO CAKES

(SERVES 6)

3 large or 4 small duck breasts

½ tsp ground cumin

½ tsp ground cinnamon

½ tsp ground ginger

½ tsp freshly ground black
   pepper

6 tbsp port

2 tsp good-quality red wine or
   sherry vinegar

*the potato cakes*

450 g/1 lb sweet potato purée,
   as dry as possible (from
   approx. 700 g/1 lb 9 oz raw
   sweet potatoes boiled in
   salted water and mashed)

1 egg, lightly beaten

2 spring onions, finely chopped

175 g/6 oz plain flour sifted
   with 2 tsp baking powder

salt and pepper

olive oil for frying

*the compote*

350 g/12 oz shallots, peeled
   and halved lengthways if
   large

25 g/1 oz butter

300 ml/10 fl oz red wine

1 heaped tbsp sugar

250 g/9 oz blackberries (tinned
   in natural juice are fine,
   drained)

▶ Score the skin of the duck breasts in diamonds approximately 1 cm/½ in across, cutting down about halfway through the layer of fat under the skin. Rub them all over with the mixed spices, massaging the spices gently into the slits. Arrange in one layer in a shallow dish and leave to marinate for 2 hours at room temperature or overnight in the fridge. If leaving in the fridge remove an hour before cooking to return to room temperature.

▶ To make the compote, put the shallots, butter, wine and sugar in a small lidded pan and cook very slowly, covered, for about 30 minutes or until the shallots are tender and covered in a sticky glaze. Add the berries to the pan and continue to cook, covered, shaking the pan occasionally for about 5 minutes or until the berries are heated through and beginning to release their juices. Set aside.

▶ To make the potato cakes, mix the potato purée with the egg and spring onion, then whisk in the flour/baking powder and season well with salt and pepper. Loosen mixture with water until it resembles pouring double cream.

▶ Heat a little olive oil in two large frying pans and drop 3 heaped tbsp separately into each pan. Use up all the batter in this way to make 18 round pancakes about 7.5 cm/3 in across. Cook, slowly turning once, until puffed and brown (be careful as they burn easily). These should be mixed and cooked just before serving.

▶ Arrange the duck breasts, skin side down in a lightly oiled heavy sauté or frying pan (non-stick would be ideal) and cook over the lowest possible heat (a heat diffuser really helps if you have one) for about 10 minutes or until little beads of blood appear on the upper, flesh side. If you want to serve the duck rare, now is the time to turn it over, but leave it for about another 2 minutes if you want it slightly more cooked but still faintly pink in the middle.

▶ Turn the breasts over on to the flesh side, turn up the heat to medium and cook for about 2 minutes or until thoroughly sealed and brown. Transfer to a warm dish and set aside. Pour off the fat from the pan.

▶ Deglaze the pan with the port and the vinegar, season with a little salt and reduce by about half until you have a syrupy consistency. Add these to the pan with the shallot mixture.

▶ To serve, slice the breasts across and arrange over the potato cakes. Top the duck with a few blackberries, then spoon the remaining compote around and serve at once.

# HONEY-GLAZED QUAIL WITH POACHED LEEKS, ROASTED ONIONS AND FLAGEOLET BEANS

Quail used to be considered a real luxury food which could only be found in game butchers and grand food departments like Harrods. Now, thankfully, these delightful little morsels are available all year round in most large supermarkets and, although they are still quite a luxury, they are not nearly as expensive as one might imagine.

One of these little birds might satisfy a dainty appetite, whereas two might be needed for a heartier one. One and a half, however, is the happy medium as you will see in the following recipe.

(SERVES 6)

9 quails
salt and pepper
3 tbsp runny honey
6 medium leeks
6 red onions
3-4 sprigs parsley
1 sprig thyme
1 bay leaf
150 ml/5 fl oz white wine
approx. 1 litre/1³/₄ pt chicken
    stock (see page 101)
extra virgin olive oil
700 g/1 lb 9 oz tinned flageolet
    beans, drained
juice of ¹/₂ lemon
2 heaped tbsp capers

► With a pair of poultry shears or kitchen scissors, cut along either side of the quails' backbones. Transfer these trimmings to a saucepan and set aside.

► Open out the quails, cut side down on a work surface and press on the breast bone with the flat of your hand to flatten.

► Now cut each in half along the breast bone, arrange these halves in one layer, cut side down in a large lightly oiled, shallow roasting tin (or baking sheet with an edge all round), season well with salt and pepper and drizzle over the honey. Refrigerate until needed.

► Trim the leeks, keeping the good green parts for the stock.

► Peel the onions, then cut across into 1 cm/¹/₂ in slices – you will need 18 slices. Keep the trimmings for the stock.

► Put the leek and onion trimmings into the saucepan with the bones. Add the herbs, wine and chicken stock to cover and simmer for an hour or two. Strain, reduce to 500 ml/18 fl oz and season with salt and pepper.

► Preheat the oven to 200°C/400°F/gas 6.

▶ Arrange the onion slices on an oiled baking sheet, brush with olive oil, season with salt and pepper and roast for about 30 minutes or until tender and browning at the edges.

▶ Roast the quail halves for about 20 minutes, basting occasionally with the honey, or until cooked through and sticky and golden looking.

▶ Cut each leek in half across and cook in boiling salted water until tender. Drain.

▶ Add the cooked beans to the reduced stock in the pan with the lemon juice, capers and 2 tbsp fruity olive oil. Reheat and season.

▶ To serve, divide the beans and their liquid between 6 large shallow soup dishes. Make a higgledy-piggledy mountain in the middle of each with the onion, leeks and quail halves (3 per serving).

# COD ROASTED IN SERRANO HAM ON HASH BROWN PARSNIPS WITH GRILLED CHICORY

(SERVES 6)

6 x thick skinless portions cod
    fillet, each weighing about
    150 g/5$^{1}/_{2}$ oz
made-up English mustard
salt and pepper
12 very thin slices Serrano ham

*the parsnips*
750 g/1 lb 10 oz parsnip,
    peeled, chopped into
    approx. 1 cm/$^{1}/_{2}$ in cubes
    and boiled until just tender
1 onion, chopped
25 g/1 oz butter
salt and pepper
olive oil

*the chicory*
6 heads chicory, trimmed and
    quartered lengthways
extra virgin olive oil
salt and pepper

*to serve*
9 tomatoes, halved, slow
    roasted with garlic and
    herbes de Provence, then
    skinned and roughly
    chopped to make a chunky
    'sauce'

▶ Preheat the oven to 220°C/425°F/gas 7.

▶ Smear the top side of each piece of fish with a very little mustard, season well with salt and pepper and wrap each neatly in 2 pieces of ham. Arrange on a lightly oiled baking sheet with the loose ends of the ham tucked neatly underneath.

▶ To make the hash browns, sauté the onion in the butter gently for 10–15 minutes or until soft and golden, then mix with the cooked parsnip, mash roughly with a fork or potato masher and season well.

▶ Tip into a lightly oiled non-stick frying pan, press down to compact, and cook over a low heat, undisturbed, for about 10 minutes or until the bottom is browned and crusty.

▶ Hold a large plate or chopping board over the pan and invert. Clean the pan if necessary, lightly oil again and slide the parsnip cake carefully back in, brown side up. Cook the other side. Cut into 6 wedges.

▶ Meanwhile brush the wedges of chicory with oil, season and cook under a preheated grill for about 15 minutes, turning frequently until beginning to char at the edges.

▶ Cook the fish parcels in the preheated oven for about 10 minutes or until the ham is crisp and the fish cooked through.

▶ To serve, arrange a fish parcel, a wedge of hash brown, 4 wedges of grilled chicory and a neat dollop of roasted tomato sauce on each large warm plate.

# Rack of Lamb with Roast Aubergine, Chick Pea and Rocket

(SERVES 6)

3 racks of lamb

salt and pepper

250 g/9 oz cooked chick peas
   (drained tinned are fine)

1 clove garlic, crushed

2 tbsp tahini paste

juice of 1 large lemon

1 tsp ground cumin

3 tbsp extra virgin olive oil

2 tbsp Greek-style yogurt

3 handfuls rocket leaves

3 small tomatoes, peeled,
   seeded, cut into long
   wedges and then these
   halved to make narrow
   triangular pieces

*the aubergine*

2 aubergines, cut across into
   approx. 1 cm/½ in slices

olive oil

salt and pepper

*the dressing*

1 tbsp white wine vinegar

1 small clove garlic, crushed

salt and pepper

4 tbsp extra virgin olive oil

▶ Preheat the oven to 200°C/400°F/gas 6.
Season the racks with salt and pepper then roast to
your liking (about 30 minutes for pinkish). Carve
into cutlets when rested.

▶ Cook the aubergine at the same time as the lamb.
Brush the slices of aubergine lightly with olive oil,
season well and arrange in one layer on lightly oiled
baking sheets. Bake for about half an hour or until
golden and cooked through.

▶ Meanwhile, roughly crush 175 g/6 oz of the chick
peas and mix with the crushed garlic, tahini, lemon
juice, cumin, olive oil and yogurt to make a chunky
humus, seasoning well with salt and pepper.

▶ Combine the dressing ingredients.

▶ To serve, spoon the humus to one side of the
plate, then make an elegant but higgledy-piggledy
pile of aubergine, rocket leaves and the remaining
chick peas and tomato triangles in the middle of the
plate. Drizzle the dressing over the salad.

▶ Lean the cutlets up against the salad with their
base in the humus.

# POACHED CHICKEN IN SAFFRON BROTH WITH POTATO 'TAGINE'

(SERVES 6)

850 ml/1½ pt reduced chicken
　　stock (see page 101 and boil
　　hard to reduce by half)
¼ tsp saffron threads
6 free-range skinless chicken
　　fillets

*the 'tagine'*
2 tbsp extra virgin olive oil
1 onion, sliced
2 level tsp ground ginger
2 level tsp ground cinnamon
2 level tsp ground cumin
2 cloves garlic, crushed
18 green olives, stoned
grated rind and juice of
　　1 lemon
500 g/1 lb 2 oz waxy potatoes,
　　cut into approx. 2 cm/
　　¾ in cubes
light chicken stock
3 tbsp cooked chick peas
　　(drained tinned are fine)

*to serve*
coriander leaves
small pieces segmented lemon
　　flesh
deep-fried sprigs of coriander
　　(optional)

▶ Sprinkle the saffron on to the reduced stock and simmer for 2–3 minutes. Add the chicken fillets and simmer for about 8 minutes or until just cooked. Cut the chicken into long thin strips and keep warm.

▶ To make the 'tagine', heat the oil in a lidded saucepan and sauté the onion for about 10 minutes or until softened but not coloured. Add the spices and continue to cook for another minute, then add the garlic, olives, lemon rind and juice and potatoes and continue to stir-fry for another minute.

▶ Add enough of the light stock to almost cover, and simmer covered for about 10 minutes. Remove the lid, add the chick peas, turn up the heat and cook, stirring, until any remaining liquid has evaporated. Do not let the mixture burn.

▶ To serve, make mountains of the potato mixture in the middle of oversized shallow soup dishes and top with a neat tangle of chicken strips.

▶ At the last moment add the coriander leaves and lemon pieces to the saffron broth and spoon around the potato mountains. Perch a deep-fried sprig of coriander on top of the chicken.

▲ Bloody Mary Gaspacho. See page 89.

▲ Spiced Chicken Risotto with Parmesan Crisps. See page 101.

# TERIYAKI BREAST OF GUINEA FOWL ON CHESTNUT RICE WITH DEEP-FRIED CABBAGE

(SERVES 6)

*the guinea fowl*

6 boneless breasts of guinea
    fowl (skin on)
6 tbsp ready-made teriyaki
    sauce (Kikkoman's is
    excellent)

*the rice*

350 g/12 oz Japanese rice
    (oriental stores and large
    supermarkets)
12 roasted chestnuts, roughly
    chopped (vacuum packed,
    frozen or tinned are fine)
425 ml/15 fl oz water
1/2 tsp salt

*the cabbage*

200 g/7 oz spring greens (or
    similar, very finely
    shredded)
oil for deep-frying
1 tsp caster sugar
salt

▶ Marinate the guinea fowl breasts in the teriyaki sauce overnight.

▶ Preheat the oven to 200°C/400°F/gas 7.

▶ Put the rice, chestnuts and water in small heavy lidded saucepan. Bring to the boil. Boil rapidly for 1 minute, then turn down the heat and cook over the lowest possible heat for about 10 minutes or until the water has been absorbed. Then leave to sit off the heat for another 10 minutes. Keep the lid tightly on the pan all the time. It will be still quite sticky even when cooked and all the water has been absorbed.

▶ Lift the breasts from the marinade and arrange in one layer, skin side up, on a lightly oiled baking sheet or shallow roasting tin and roast at the top of the oven for 10–15 minutes or until cooked through, brushing the skin a couple of times with more teriyaki sauce. Slice the breasts across into bite-sized pieces.

▶ At the last minute briefly deep-fry the greens in small batches until crisp, drain well and sprinkle with the sugar and a little salt.

▶ To serve, divide the rice between 6 large warm plates and spread out to make a wide even disc. Put mounds of cabbage in the centre, leaving a border of rice, and perch the slices of breast on top, glazed skin side up.

# Ribbons of Trout in Beer Batter with Japanese Buckwheat Noodles and Mushroom Broth

(Serves 6)

6 skinless fillets of trout, each
    weighing approx. 150 g/
    5¹/₂ oz
Japanese wasabe paste
    (oriental grocers and large
    supermarkets)
oil for deep-frying

*the batter*
200 g/7 oz plain flour
330 ml/11 fl oz lager

*the broth*
1.5 litres/2³/₄ pt chicken stock
    (see page 101)
1 tbsp sliced fresh ginger
2 whole cloves garlic
2 tbsp Kikkoman soy sauce

*to serve*
350 g/12 oz Japanese
    buckwheat noodles
500 g/1 lb 2 oz assorted
    mushrooms, sautéed in a
    little butter
chopped chives (not too fine)
oriental sesame oil

▶ To make the broth put the stock, ginger and garlic in a pan, reduce by half, strain and add the soy sauce.

▶ Just before serving, make a batter with the flour and lager. It should be the consistency of thick single cream.

▶ Smear a mere trace of wasabe paste over one side of the fish fillets, then cut them across into approximately 1 cm/¹/₂ in strips, dip in the batter and deep-fry until crisp and golden.

▶ Meanwhile cook the noodles according to the instructions on the packet. Drain well.

▶ To serve, make mountains of hot cooked noodles in the centre of over-sized shallow soup dishes. Scatter the cooked mushrooms around and pour over the broth. Pile the battered fish strips on top of the noodles.

▶ Scatter the chopped chives around the dish on to the broth, and sprinkle with a few drops of sesame oil.

# HELTER-SKELTER DUCK AND FILO PARCELS

When asked for my favourite restaurant, I generally reply 'most of the restaurants in Sydney', as I spend a month in Australia every winter. In South London, however, where I live for most of the year, I am very fortunate to have an excellent restaurant, Helter Skelter, right in the middle of Brixton within 10 minutes' walk. Run by John and Natasha Swerdlov, the food is so good I can imagine I am in Sydney. John kindly gave me this recipe.

(SERVES **6** AS A FIRST COURSE)

**1 oven-ready duckling, weighing approx. 2 kg/ 4¹/₂ lb**
**salt and pepper**
**100 g/3¹/₂ oz unsalted butter**
**2 crisp dessert apples, peeled, cored and diced**
**1 bunch spring onions, chopped**
**4 heaped tbsp chopped fresh coriander**
**¹/₂ tsp Chinese 5-spice powder (supermarkets)**
**1 tbsp runny honey**
**12 sheets filo pastry (thawed if frozen – but fresh is best if you can get it)**
**sesame seeds**

*to serve*
**salad leaves or a simple cucumber salad**
**hoi sin sauce**

▶ Preheat the oven to 230°C/450°F/gas 8.

▶ Prick the skin of the duck all over with a skewer and then season well with salt and pepper, rubbing it well into the skin. Arrange the duck on a rack over a roasting tin and roast for 20 minutes. Turn the heat down to 190°C/375°F/gas 5 and continue to roast for another 30 minutes. Remove from the oven and allow to cool. Strip the meat from the bones, discarding the skin, and cut into small bite-sized pieces (the carcass will make superb stock).

▶ Heat half the butter in a wok or frying pan and stir-fry the apples for about 5 minutes. In a bowl mix with the meat, spring onions, coriander, 5-spice, honey and seasoning.

▶ Melt the remaining butter and preheat the oven to 220°C/425°F/gas 7.

▶ Lay a sheet of filo on the work surface, place about 2 heaped tbsp of the duck mixture in the centre and brush around the edges with melted butter. Then fold in the sides then the top and bottom edges. Brush another sheet of filo with butter, place the parcel seam side down in the centre and repeat the wrapping action.

▶ Make another 5 parcels in the same way and arrange seams down on a lightly oiled baking sheet. Brush with butter, sprinkle with sesame seeds and bake for 15–20 minutes or until crisp and golden. Serve on large plates with salad and hoi sin sauce.

# PUFF PASTRY ORIGAMI BASKETS OF GARLIC MUSHROOMS WITH ASPARAGUS SAUCE

This is my favourite recipe for getting oohs and aahs when I do demonstrations. It is so easy to achieve once you have learned the knack of folding the pastry basket and is always very impressive. Slightly pretentious (like me), it has become almost a signature dish.

You can make extra pastry baskets and freeze them ready to be heated through and filled with all kinds of fillings sweet or savoury.

I use sheets of ready-rolled puff pastry which you can buy in large supermarkets. Cut the trimmings into even shapes and cook them separately to serve with stews and casseroles.

(SERVES 6 AS A SUBSTANTIAL STARTER OR LIGHT MAIN COURSE)

**the baskets**

6 x 20 cm/8 in thinly rolled
     squares puff pastry (see
     above)
1 egg yolk mixed with 1 tbsp
     milk to glaze

**the filling**

75 g/2¾ oz unsalted butter
350 g/12 oz button mushrooms,
     sliced if not tiny
2 cloves garlic, crushed
1 heaped tbsp finely chopped
     parsley
salt and pepper

**the sauce**

24 small/medium stalks of
     asparagus, bottom third
     trimmed away
300 ml/10 fl oz single cream
salt and pepper

▶ Preheat the oven to 200°C/400°F/gas 6.

▶ To make the baskets, brush the pastry squares on one side with the egg mixture. Using a sharp knife make cuts 2.5 cm/1 in from the edges of each square, stopping 3 cm/1¼ in short of two opposing corners (see diagram). Bring one cut edge over and place along the opposite inside corner of the square, then repeat with the other side. (This sounds very complicated but as the diagram shows is actually very simple.) Brush the unglazed edges with the egg yolk mixture.

▶ Bake for about 15 minutes or until puffed and golden. Poke the middle of the baskets down with the end of a wooden spoon to make plenty of room for the filling.

▶ Meanwhile heat the butter in a wok or frying pan and stir-fry the mushrooms with the garlic and parsley until tender. Season with salt and pepper.

▶ Cut the tips from the asparagus and boil in salted water for 2–3 minutes until just tender, then drain.

▶ Boil the remaining asparagus stem portions in another pan of salted water for 6–7 minutes or until really tender, then liquidise with the cream, seasoning with salt and pepper. Return this sauce to the pan and reheat.

▶ To serve, arrange the baskets filled with mushrooms on warmed plates, and surround with the sauce and four asparagus tips.

# ROAST CRUMBED FILLET OF BEEF

My mother served roast fillet of beef for my twenty-first birthday dinner party, and since then it has always been one of my favourite meals. It is a very expensive treat and as it is a very lean cut of beef is ruined even more than other cuts by overcooking. So if you don't like your beef very rare ignore this recipe and choose something else to cook.

With a treat like this, simplicity is the essence, but the crisp crumb coating really does add a little extra dimension to what might already seem perfect.

(SERVES 6)

1 neatly tied joint of fillet of
   beef weighing approx.
   1 kg/2¼ lb
seasoned flour
1 egg beaten with 1 tbsp milk
fresh fine white breadcrumbs
   (made from slightly stale
   bread)
extra virgin olive oil

▶ Remove the meat from the fridge at least 1 hour before cooking to bring to room temperature. *This is of paramount importance.*

▶ Preheat the oven to 230°C/450°F/gas 8.

▶ Roll the beef first in flour, then egg mix, then breadcrumbs, shaking off the excess each time.

▶ Sit in a lightly oiled roasting tin, drizzle sparingly but evenly with olive oil and roast for 20 minutes. Remove from the oven and leave to rest for 20 minutes before carving. The resting time is as important as the cooking time as it allows the muscle to 'relax' after the 'shock' of the hot oven, and the juices to redistribute themselves throughout the meat resulting in tender juicy beef. Carve in thickish slices (2–3 per portion).

▶ Serve with the simplest of accompaniments. We are not talking 'meat and two veg' here! In winter I would choose mashed carrots and swede with lots of butter and black pepper and in high summer I would arrange the warm slices of beef on a simple bed of perfect ripe tomato slices, with a little of my best 'extra virgin', plus a perfect simple green salad and a glass of the best red wine I could afford. I can never decide whether I prefer mustard or horseradish so I always offer a choice.

# CHAPTER 6

# TEN FAST FAB FEASTS

Readers and viewers often tell me that, although they love to cook, one of the things they find difficult, particularly when cooking a special meal, is choosing a well-balanced menu. As a result, I have grouped the remainder of the recipes in this book as such.

There are menus for all kinds of occasion from the most informal weekend brunch to decidedly posh dinner parties. All, however, are easy to shop for, and carefully planned in order that the cook doesn't have to spend hours and hours cooking so that he or she is worn out before the guests arrive and too tired to enjoy the fruits of their labour.

Adapt these menus as you would recipes, to suit your own personal tastes and needs. Swap the courses around at will, or substitute a simpler or ready-made first course or pudding if time is short.

I spend so many hours in my kitchen testing recipes for 'work' and although I never tire of cooking, when it comes to preparing a meal for friends, although I want it to be really delicious (they expect it!), I want to be in and out of the kitchen as quickly as possible. I don't want to rush, and I want to be able to enjoy the task in hand. I do!

*PS One final but invaluable tip is – to work out how long you think it is going to take to prepare a meal, and then allow at least another half an hour. You will be surprised how much more you enjoy your cooking and how much better your food turns out.*

## MENU 1

# A BRILLIANT BRUNCH

Why not entertain American style with a brunch party and invite friends (and their dogs?) around late on Sunday morning for an informal hearty meal. A huge bowl of fresh fruit will round the meal off perfectly.

Serve a selection of teas and coffee plus whatever alcohol you fancy (champagne is always perfect), and provide all the Sunday papers.

# BANANA LEMON YOGURT SMOOTHIE

 Smoothies are the perfect instant breakfast (or anytime snack) for those who don't like breakfast, and are a great lazy way of eating fruit. The best thing is that although they are very healthy they taste incredibly creamy and decadent. Unless you have an enormous food processor or blender you may need to make this in batches.

(SERVES 6)

3 large bananas

3 tbsp lemon juice

3 tbsp honey

425 ml/15 fl oz low-fat natural
    yogurt

425 ml/15 fl oz milk

*to garnish (optional)*
**lemon slices and/or sprigs of
    fresh mint**

▶ Place all the ingredients in the bowl of a food processor or liquidiser and blend until smooth (see above).

▶ To serve, pour into glasses and garnish with lemon slices and mint leaves if used.

# Bloody Mary Gazpacho

Based on a combination of two classic recipes, this potent little chilled soup is served in quite small quantities.

(SERVES **6**)
**500 ml/18 fl oz tomato juice**
**1 small clove garlic, crushed**
**juice of 1 lime (or to taste)**
**4 tbsp vodka (or more or less**
**to taste)**
**2 tbsp Worcestershire sauce, or**
**more to taste**
**salt and pepper**
**4 ripe tomatoes, finely chopped**
**(peeled and deseeded if you**
**have time)**
**¹/₃ cucumber, deseeded and**
**finely chopped (leave the**
**skin on)**
**¹/₂ small mild onion, finely**
**chopped**
**1 green pepper, deseeded and**
**finely chopped**
**2 sticks celery, finely chopped**

*the croûtons*
**2 slices white bread, crusts**
**removed and cut into**
**approximately 1 cm/¹/₂ in**
**cubes, then fried crisp in a**
**little extra virgin olive oil**

▶ Pour the tomato juice into a bowl and stir in the garlic, lime juice, vodka and Worcestershire sauce. Season well with salt and pepper. Chill for at least 4 hours or overnight.

▶ About 1 hour before serving, stir about three-quarters of the chopped vegetables into the Bloody Mary mixture and return to the fridge.

▶ To serve, divide the chilled mixture between 6 small bowls, glasses or cups, pile the remaining vegetables on top and scatter with croûtons.

# EGGS BENEDICT

Many people find poaching eggs very difficult, as they sometimes 'spread' in a messy fashion when dropped into the water. Firstly, you must use the freshest of eggs (many supermarkets sell eggs with the date of packing on the box). The little known 'secret' of cooking them for a minute in their shell first really helps them keep their shape and almost guarantees success every time. Hollandaise sauce is tricky to make, so don't be afraid to use a packet (there are some good ones around now – Schwartz's is good).

(SERVES 6)

6 very fresh eggs (see above)

6 slices cooked ham

6 muffins, toasted

hollandaise sauce (see above), made according to the instructions on the packet

► Fill a bowl with just boiled water, put in the eggs in their shells and leave for exactly 1 minute. Then carefully crack into a frying pan of gently simmering water. The water should be barely trembling. As soon as they are cooked to your liking (about 3 minutes for set white and runny yolk), remove from the pan with a fish slice.

► Meanwhile put the ham on top of the freshly toasted muffins and have them by the cooker on warmed plates.

► Sit the poached eggs on top of the ham, pour over the hot sauce (as much or as little as you fancy) and serve at once.

# SMOKED TROUT AND QUAIL EGG KEDGEREE

A wonderful traditional English breakfast dish, originally invented by British Colonials in India. Those were the days, however, when you had servants to make you breakfast and as I don't have any myself, I find this dish much more suitable for brunch, lunch or dinner.

**(SERVES 6)**
24 hard-boiled quail eggs (boil 3 minutes)
500 g/1 lb 2 oz long-grain rice (preferably basmati)
100 g/3½ oz butter
2 small onions, chopped
2 tsp Indian curry powder (or to taste)
250 g/9 oz smoked trout, skinned and flaked
2 tbsp chopped parsley
juice of ½ lemon
salt and pepper

▶ Shell the eggs. Leave 12 whole and cut the remainder in half to show the yolks.

▶ Boil the rice according to the instructions on the packet, drain and return to the pan.

▶ Melt the butter in a pan and stir-fry the onion with the curry powder over a medium heat for 8–10 minutes until soft and transparent but not coloured.

▶ Stir this into the rice with the fish, eggs, half the parsley and the lemon juice, stir together thoroughly and season to taste with salt and pepper if necessary.

▶ Stir the mixture over a moderate heat until piping hot (alternatively transfer to a serving dish, cover with foil and heat through in a moderate oven for 10–15 minutes), pile on to a hot plate and serve garnished with the remaining parsley.

# Menu 2
# Stand-up Eats

Drinks parties are a great way to entertain a crowd, but unless you and your guests are definitely going on for 'dinner', it is important that 'nibbles' should be rather more than that, and should really constitute a proper meal.

Most of the preparation for these dishes (even the two hot ones) can be done well in advance, leaving the cook free to enjoy the party with everyone else. If you want to make the meal more substantial simply add an assortment of crudités with dips, plus some nuts and olives – and a big platter of hot sausages simply cooked in the oven will always be welcome as the party comes to a close.

# Sesame Prawn Tostinis

Everyone loves these incredibly tasty savoury morsels, but the normal Chinese restaurant version, being deep-fried, is simply oozing unwanted calories. This version, being fat-free, is considerably lower in calories and tastes if anything even better than the fried version.

Uncooked prawns, with the shells on but the heads removed, are available frozen from fishmongers and large supermarkets.

(SERVES 12)

350 g/12 oz raw prawns (see above), thawed and shells removed

50 g/1¾ oz tinned water chestnuts, drained

50 g/1¾ oz lean cooked ham

¾ tsp salt

1 heaped tsp cornflour

white of 1 large egg

9 small thin slices white bread, crusts removed

2 tbsp sesame seeds (or as needed)

▶ Preheat the oven to 220°C/425°F/gas 7.
Put the first 6 ingredients in the bowl of a liquidiser or food processor and reduce to a smooth purée, then divide between the slices of bread, spreading evenly. Sprinkle over the sesame seeds to cover, patting them in gently.

▶ Arrange the slices of bread on a non-stick baking sheet and bake for 6–7 minutes, or until the bread is crisp. Arrange under a hot grill for a few seconds to ensure the sesame seeds are a nice golden brown. Cut each slice into 4 fingers.

▶ To serve, transfer to a serving plate and hand round straight from the oven.

# CURRIED GARLIC AND PARMESAN MUSSELS

Most of the work in this recipe can be done well before the party, and all you have to do is pop the stuffed mussels in the oven for a few minutes just before serving.

(SERVES 12)

70-80 mussels (approximately
    1 kg/2¼ lb)
85 g/3 oz Parmesan cheese,
    freshly grated
3 tbsp finely chopped parsley
4 heaped tbsp fine fresh white
    breadcrumbs
60 g/2¼ oz softened butter
2 cloves garlic, crushed
2 tsp curry powder
salt and pepper

▶ Clean the mussels as described on page 41. The mussels are now ready to be opened. Place them in a dry pan, cover it and simply turn on the heat to medium. The pan will not burn because when the mussels open, they release quite a lot of their own liquid.

▶ Cook for 3–4 minutes, shaking the pan occasionally. Remove the lid and, as the mussels open, take them out of the pan. It is important to take them out as they open because they will become tough and rubbery if allowed to cook for too long. Any that stubbornly refuse to open should be discarded. Remove and discard half the shell from each mussel.

▶ Preheat the oven to 225°C/425°F/gas 7. Mix the Parmesan, parsley, breadcrumbs, butter, garlic and curry powder together and season generously with salt and pepper. Use the mixture to 'stuff' the mussels, spooning a little on to each one in its shell.

▶ Arrange the mussels in one layer in a suitable roasting tin or shallow ovenproof dish. Place in the oven and cook only until the 'stuffing' has melted and the mussels feel hot to the touch. This will take 10–15 minutes. Do not overcook or the mussels will soon become tough and rubbery.

▶ To serve, transfer to a platter and hand round immediately.

# Scotch Quail Eggs

 These are much easier to make than you might imagine and very impressive. They rely for success on really flavoursome sausage meat. Rather than rely on what might be bland sausage meat in a supermarket packet I buy the best-quality sausages I can find and remove the skin.

(MAKES 12)

12 quail eggs, hard-boiled
    (3 minutes) and shelled
350 g/12 oz (or a bit more if
    needed) sausagemeat (see
    above)
seasoned flour
2 eggs, beaten
fine fresh white breadcrumbs
vegetable oil for deep-frying

▶ Carefully mould about 25 g/1 oz of sausagemeat around each egg, making sure there are no gaps. Then dip each one in flour, then beaten egg, then breadcrumbs, shaking off the excess each time.

▶ Deep-fry the eggs in hot oil for about 5 minutes or until crisp and golden. Drain on kitchen paper and allow to cool.

▶ To serve, slice each egg in half.

# Olive Palmiers

These very impressive little savoury biscuits are not at all difficult to make, but they do take a little time. They can however be made the day before, stored in an airtight container and then reheated for a few minutes to make them really crisp just before serving. Tapenade is a savoury olive paste which is available in small jars from delicatessens and good supermarkets.

(MAKES 36–40 BISCUITS)

370 g/13 oz puff pastry,
    thawed if frozen
2 tbsp tapenade (see above), or
    more if needed
1 egg, lightly beaten

▶ Preheat the oven to 200°C/400°F/gas 6.

▶ Roll the pastry out to make a rectangle measuring approximately 20 x 30 cm/8 x 12 in. Trim if necessary to make the sides nice and straight and discard the trimmings. Cut this rectangle in half lengthways.

▶ Spread 1 tbsp of tapenade down the centre of each pastry strip, leaving a plain border, a quarter width of the strip, down each side. Fold these plain borders in to meet in the centre, brush with beaten egg and fold lengthways in half once more, so that the egg-brushed areas stick together. Now brush all the remaining surfaces of the 'roll' with beaten egg and cut across into 1 cm/½ in slices. Press each lightly with the palm of the hand (hence the name 'palmier'!) to flatten slightly.

▶ Arrange these on a lightly oiled baking sheet, allowing plenty of room between each one as they will spread to about 3 times their size as they cook. Bake for 10–12 minutes or until brown and crisp.

▶ To serve, transfer to a serving plate and serve fresh from the oven.

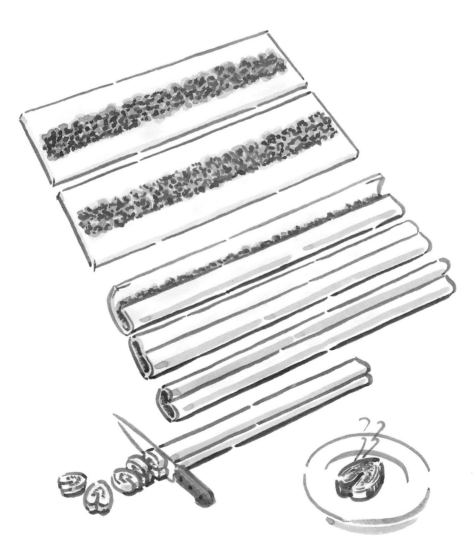

# GOAT'S CHEESE AND PINE KERNEL 'TRUFFLES'

The ideal goat's cheese to use for these incredibly savoury little mouthfuls is the French chèvres cut from a log sold by weight, and available in most delicatessens and cheese shops. As a variation use olive oil instead of walnut and add a small clove of crushed garlic.

(SERVES 12)

350 g/12 oz goat's cheese (see above)

2 tbsp walnut oil

salt and pepper

350 g/12 oz pine kernels, 'toasted' light golden in a hot, dry, non-stick frying pan

▶ Put the cheese in a bowl and mash with a fork, pour over the oil and season with salt and pepper. Mix well.

▶ Put the pine kernels into a shallow bowl. Form the cheese mixture into small balls – about 2 cm/¾ in across – then roll in the pine kernels until completely coated. Arrange in one layer on a large plate and chill for at least 1 hour or up to 24 to firm up.

▶ To serve, arrange in a pyramid on an attractive serving plate.

▲ Roast Ham-wrapped Asparagus. See page 108.

▲ Roast Cherry Tomatoes with Garlic and Twiggy Herbs. See page 111.

## Menu 3

# Central Eating for Winter

Beefy stews and casseroles have been rather out of fashion for some time now, perhaps because of the modern obsession with eating less red meat, and serving light and 'pretty' food. It is indeed difficult to arrange this kind of food prettily on a plate (although I think it is very chic to serve it in wide soup plates). We also tend to think of slow-cooked dishes as only suitable for everyday eating, whereas the French love to serve this kind of food for winter celebrations. This very British menu is based around exactly such a dish.

# Pear and Walnut Salad with Stilton Dressing

This is one of those flavour combinations made in heaven, and the best in my opinion of all the fruit and cheese matchings.

Stilton is still made only in a small designated area of the country in much the same way that champagne can only come from Champagne.

It is wonderful that we can now get top-quality apples and pears all year round with New World countries like New Zealand producing excellent fruit in our 'reverse' season. William pears would be my choice if you can get them or Taylor's Gold from New Zealand – but any fragrant ripe variety will do.

**(SERVES 6 AS A FIRST COURSE)**

**6 ripe pears, peeled, cored and sliced lengthways at the last minute**

**75 g/2¾ oz walnut halves**

**1 bag mixed salad leaves**

*the dressing*
**100 g/3½ oz Stilton**
**1 tbsp single cream or milk**
**1 tbsp white wine vinegar**
**3 tbsp vegetable oil**
**salt and pepper**

▶ First make the dressing. In a bowl, mash the cheese thoroughly with the cream/milk to make a smooth paste, then whisk in the vinegar and oil. Season to taste, but go steady with the salt as the cheese is already quite salty. If the dressing is a little too thick, whisk in a little more cream/milk.

▶ To serve, arrange 'nests' of leaves on 6 large plates, and scatter over the pear slices and the walnuts. Drizzle over the dressing and serve at once.

# BEEF IN GUINNESS WITH GREMOLATA

This recipe is quite delicious enough to serve for a special occasion with the added advantage that it is so simple to cook. There is no need for dipping things in messy flour or frying in advance. This recipe uses only one pot and is prepared with almost no effort in three stages over three days. The first day, all the ingredients are chucked in the pot and left to marinate. Next day they are cooked slowly for several hours until the meat is meltingly tender, then left overnight for the flavours to develop and for any unwanted fat to come to the top and be discarded, leaving only a brief spell in the oven at the last minute to heat through.

(SERVES 6)

1.25 kg/2³/₄ lb lean stewing or
    casserole beef, cubed
2 onions, chopped
2 cloves garlic, crushed
1 large carrot, cut across into
    1 cm/¹/₂ in sections
1 stick celery, chopped
200 g/7 oz mushrooms, sliced
    if large
1 tbsp sugar
3 bay leaves
finely pared peel of ¹/₂ orange
3-4 sprigs fresh thyme (or
    1 tsp dried)
2 tbsp extra virgin olive oil
salt and pepper
600 ml/1 pt Guinness
1 tbsp cornflour mixed with a
    little water

the gremolata
3 tbsp chopped parsley
2 cloves garlic, very finely
    chopped
finely grated rind of 1 lemon

▶ Place all the ingredients for the stew, except the cornflour mixture, in a large lidded ovenproof casserole, and leave to marinate for 24 hours.

▶ Preheat the oven to 160°C/325°F/gas 3.

▶ Cook the casserole in the oven, covered, for 1 hour, by which time it should be bubbling. Turn down the heat to 150°C/300°F/gas 2, and continue to cook for about 3 hours or until the meat is really tender.

▶ Allow to cool, then chill for at least 8 hours or preferably overnight. With a small spoon carefully remove and discard any fat from the top of the meat mixture, fish out and discard the orange peel and bay leaves, then stir in the cornflour mixture.

▶ Reheat at 190°C/375°F/gas 5 for about 45–60 minutes when needed. The gravy should be quite thin, but if you would like it a bit thicker add another tbsp of cornflour dissolved in a couple of tbsp of the gravy. Stir this quickly in off the heat, then return to the oven for another 10 minutes.

▶ Combine the gremolata ingredients.

▶ Serve the casserole in heated wide soup bowls sprinkled with a little gremolata, perhaps with buttered noodles and one green vegetable.

# IRISH COFFEE ICE CREAM WITH HOT TOFFEE SAUCE

 This ice cream is really a parfait, which is my favourite kind of iced dessert, because once made, you simply put it into the freezer and leave it – no need to stir, no need for a machine, and it will never freeze too hard.
You do need an electric whisk, however, but a hand-held one is perfect.

(SERVES 6)
**5 free-range medium egg yolks
syrup made by boiling
    125 g/4¹/₂ oz sugar with
    150 ml/5 fl oz very strong
    black coffee for 3 minutes
300 ml/10 fl oz double cream
3 tbsp Irish whiskey**

▶ Whisk the egg yolks (see above) until light and fluffy, about 2 minutes. Then, still whisking, pour on the hot (just off the boil) syrup and continue to whisk until the mixture has at least doubled in volume, and is the consistency of whipped cream just before it will make stiff peaks. This takes 5–10 minutes.

▶ Next whip the cream with the whiskey until it holds soft peaks, then fold into the egg yolk mixture. Transfer to a freezer-proof container and freeze for at least 6 hours.

▶ To serve, transfer from the freezer to the fridge about 15 minutes before required then serve with the following sauce.

# HOT TOFFEE SAUCE

This wickedly delicious sauce is very simple to make and is good poured hot or cold over all kinds of ice creams – or other puddings.

(SERVES 6)
**50 g/1³/₄ oz butter
50 g/1³/₄ oz soft brown sugar
2 tbsp golden syrup
150 ml/5 fl oz single cream**

▶ Put the first three ingredients in a small saucepan and heat gently, stirring, until the butter and sugar have melted. Turn up the heat and boil hard for 3 minutes. Allow to cool a little and then stir in the cream.

MENU 4

# MELTING POT POURRI

This eclectic menu not only tastes totally fab, but gives you a round-the-world tour without expensive air tickets and jet-lag.

# GREEN BEAN, CHICK PEA AND SESAME SALAD

 This is very loosely adapted from a Japanese recipe with a bit of Mediterranean tahini (sesame paste) thrown in. To make it more substantial you could add a few cooked peeled prawns, but I like it just as it is.
This dressing is also delicious with other cooked vegetables, like spinach and other greens, and asparagus and broccoli.
Toasted sesame seeds are such a useful flavour-adder to all kinds of food (simply sprinkle on top of rice, noodles or vegetables) that it is worth toasting more than required for this recipe (but use within 2 days).

(SERVES 6)
500 g/1 lb 2 oz green beans,
    ends snapped off
salt
1 x 420 g tin chick peas,
    drained and rinsed

*the sesame dressing*
2 tbsp tahini (delicatessens and
    large supermarkets)
2 tbsp Kikkoman soy sauce
juice of 1 lime (2 tbsp)
1 tbsp soft dark brown sugar

*to garnish*
3 tbsp sesame seeds

▶ Parboil the green beans in lightly salted water until just barely cooked and still crisp, about 4 minutes (time depends on size of bean). Plunge into cold water to cool and arrest cooking. Drain and cut into 5 cm/2 in lengths.

▶ Combine the dressing ingredients in a bowl, then add the beans and chick peas and toss well to coat.

▶ Meanwhile, 'toast' the sesame seeds until pale golden in a hot dry frying pan.

▶ Serve the salad at room temperature sprinkled liberally with sesame seeds.

# SPICED CHICKEN RISOTTO WITH PARMESAN CRISPS

This is inspired by a totally memorable risotto I ate in Assisi. It might seem a dauntingly long recipe, but it's not. Once the ingredients are assembled it is dead easy, as the stock is made the day before. After you have made a proper risotto you will become quite addicted to this pleasurable and very satisfying process.

(SERVES 6)

*the chicken and stock*

1 free-range chicken, weighing
   about 2 kg/4¹/₂ lb
1 onion, unskinned, quartered
1 large leek, cleaned and
   roughly chopped
2 whole cloves garlic, peeled
1 carrot, roughly chopped
1 stick celery, roughly chopped
1 x 5 cm/2 in strip lemon peel
2 bay leaves
1 good bunch parsley
2-3 sprigs thyme
1 tsp salt
2 grinds of black pepper

*the risotto*

1 tbsp extra virgin olive oil
75 g/2¹/₂ oz unsalted butter
1 onion, chopped
1 large clove garlic, crushed
425 g/15 oz risotto rice
1.5 litres/2³/₄ pt chicken stock
150 ml/5 fl oz dry white wine
25 g/1 oz raisins
1 heaped tsp curry powder
salt and pepper

*the crisps*

150 g/5¹/₂ oz Parmesan cheese,
   freshly grated

▶ Begin the day before. Put the chicken and stock ingredients in a large saucepan and add cold water to just cover (about 2 litres/3¹/₂ pt), bring to the boil and simmer, covered, for 30 minutes. Remove from the heat, and leave undisturbed for 45 minutes. By this time the chicken will be perfectly cooked with tender moist flesh.

▶ Lift the chicken out and cut the meat from the bones, removing the skin. Cut or tear the meat into bite-sized pieces and refrigerate until needed.

▶ Return the skin and bones to the pan and simmer, covered, for another hour, then strain into a bowl discarding the solids. Chill overnight, when all the fat will come to the surface and solidify so that it can be carefully removed and discarded.

▶ To make the risotto heat the oil and half the butter in a large pan and stir-fry the onion over a medium heat for 5–10 minutes or until soft and transparent. Add the garlic and rice and continue to stir-fry for 2–3 minutes.

▶ Bring the stock to the boil in another pan and keep warm over a low heat.

▶ Add the wine and raisins to the rice and cook over a medium heat, stirring occasionally, until the liquid has been absorbed.

▼ ▶ Ladle just enough hot stock over the rice to cover.

Continue to cook over a medium heat, stirring occasionally, until the liquid has been absorbed, then add another ladleful of stock. Never add more stock than will just cover the rice. Continue this process until all the stock has been used and the rice is cooked, 20–25 minutes.

▶ Depending on the rice, you may not use all the stock. On the other hand, you may use it all up before the rice is cooked, in which case continue adding boiling water instead of stock.

▶ The finished risotto should be moist and creamy with a little bite left in the centre of each grain of rice.

▶ Approximately 3–4 minutes before it is cooked stir in the remaining butter, the curry powder (the curry flavour should be very subtle) and the chicken pieces.

▶ While the risotto is cooking make the Parmesan crisps. Preheat the oven to 200°C/400°F/gas 6.

▶ Line 2–3 baking sheets with non-stick kitchen parchment and spoon on tablespoonfuls of grated Parmesan spreading them out to make circles approximately 10 cm/4 in across (leave a little gap between each). Bake for 7–10 minutes or until the cheese has melted into lacey discs by which time they will have hardened completely. Remove from the tray with a spatula or fish slice and set aside. Repeat in batches until you have made 12 crisps.

▶ Serve the risotto in warm soup bowls with the Parmesan crisps either arranged on top or to the side.

# Pear and Almond Tart

(SERVES 6)

300 g/10$^1$/$_2$ oz shortcrust pastry
    (thawed if frozen)
approx. 450 g/1 lb pears
    (3–4 depending on size),
    peeled, cored and sliced
    lengthways at the last
    minute

*the frangipane filling*
100 g/3$^1$/$_2$ oz unsalted butter
100 g/3$^1$/$_2$ oz caster sugar
1 egg and 1 egg yolk
2 tsp Cointreau, or other fruit
    liqueur or brandy (or
    orange juice)
100 g/3$^1$/$_2$ oz ground almonds
50 g/1$^3$/$_4$ oz flour

*to garnish*
1 tbsp flaked almonds
apricot jam (melted and
    strained to make a glaze)

▶ Preheat the oven to 200°C/400°F/gas 6.

▶ Roll out the pastry and line a 20–23 cm/8–9 in loose-bottomed tart tin. Chill for 30 minutes.

▶ Meanwhile make the frangipane filling. Cream the butter and sugar until pale, then beat in the eggs and alcohol (or orange juice) followed by the ground almonds and flour. Pour into the chilled pastry case and arrange the pear slices on top like the spokes of a wheel, narrow ends to the centre.

▶ Bake for 10–15 minutes until the pastry begins to brown at the edges, then turn down the heat to 180°C/350°F/gas 4 and continue to cook for another 15–20 minutes or until the frangipane is set. About 10 minutes before the tart is cooked sprinkle with the almonds.

▶ Allow to cool, then brush with apricot glaze.

▶ Serve at room temperature with whipped cream, vanilla ice cream or natural yogurt.

## MENU 5

# ORIENT EXPRESS

Take a trip around the Far East in this collection of recipes carefully adapted to be quick and easy to prepare using only ingredients from your local supermarket.

# THAI PRAWN SALAD

Although the list of ingredients in this recipe may seem a little daunting, don't be put off because, once assembled, you simply throw them together. You will find everything you need in any large supermarket, at any time of the year, including the fresh herbs, tinned water chestnuts and oriental fish sauce. This is a clear, pungent condiment used in many oriental cuisines.

(SERVES 6)

500 g/1 lb 2 oz large cooked shelled prawns

3 small sticks celery

1 red onion

1 red or yellow pepper

150 g/5½ oz drained tinned water chestnuts

2 fresh red or green chillies

250 g/9 oz seedless grapes (any colour), halved

75 g/2¾ oz toasted flaked almonds

3 tbsp coriander leaves

3 heaped tsp chopped mint

the dressing

1 clove garlic, crushed

1 rounded tbsp sugar

3 tbsp oriental fish sauce

juice of 2 limes

2 tbsp water

a dash of Tabasco sauce

▶ To prepare the vegetables, cut the celery into small batons. Chop or thinly slice the onion. Deseed the pepper and cut into small narrow strips. Halve the water chestnuts to make thin discs. Deseed and finely chop the chillies.

▶ Combine the dressing ingredients in one bowl and the salad ingredients in another, and chill for up to 3 hours or until needed.

▶ Just before serving pour the dressing over the salad, toss well and divide between 6 plates or bowls.

# WONTON SOUP

One of the all-time favourite classics of Chinese cuisine, this substantial soup is much loved the world over.

For the soup itself all you need is some excellent chicken stock (see page 101). Wonton skins are available from all oriental grocers, usually in the freezer, and once thawed the rest only takes minutes. Or you can simply buy ready-made wontons, which are available frozen from oriental grocers. Use Chinese greens, or baby spinach, shredded lettuce, watercress etc.

(SERVES 6)

*the wontons*

75 g/2 ¾ oz minced chicken or turkey

115 g/4 oz sausagemeat

1 tbsp dry sherry

½ tsp ginger juice (squeeze fresh ginger through a garlic press)

1 tbsp egg white (white of 1 small egg)

36 wonton skins (thawed if frozen)

*the soup*

1.75 litres/3 pt good chicken stock (see page 101)

125 g/4½ oz tender greens (see above)

*to serve*

3 spring onions, thinly sliced

oriental sesame oil

▶ Make the wontons. Thoroughly combine the first 5 ingredients, then put 1 tsp of this mixture into the centre of each skin and bring up the edges to form little sacks, sealing with a drop of water.

▶ Bring the chicken stock to the boil in a big pan (roomy enough to take the wontons without overcrowding). Add the wontons and greens and simmer for 3–5 minutes or until the wontons rise to the surface.

▶ To serve, divide between 6 heated bowls and sprinkle each serving with the spring onions and a few drops of sesame oil.

# Green Chicken Curry

 My simplified variation of a Thai-style curry, this still does, however, rely on using Thai green curry paste and oriental fish sauce. These are now happily available not just in oriental food shops but in most large supermarkets. I use green curry paste made by Bart Spices which is excellent.
The real bonus of this fragrant dish is that it is gloriously simple and quick to make. Serve with noodles or Thai jasmine rice.

(SERVES **4–6** DEPENDING ON THE REST
   OF THE MEAL)

1 tbsp vegetable oil

2 tbsp green curry paste (see
   above)

4 boneless chicken breast
   fillets, cut across into
   approx. 1 cm/½ in slices

2 tbsp oriental fish sauce (see
   above)

½ x 400 ml tin coconut milk
   (available from
   supermarkets)

115 g/4 oz frozen peas

1 bunch spring onions, trimmed
   and cut into long shreds

2 medium green chillies (or
   more to taste), deseeded
   (unless you want a really
   hot dish), and shredded

2 heaped tbsp chopped fresh
   coriander

▶ Heat a wok or large sauté pan, then add the oil and stir-fry the curry paste for 1 minute or until it becomes fragrant.

▶ Add the chicken and fish sauce and stir-fry for another 3–4 minutes or until the chicken is just cooked.

▶ Add the coconut milk (save the rest of the milk for another day, or pour over tropical fruit for an alternative pudding), and bring to the boil. Add the peas and continue to cook just until the peas are heated through.

▶ Combine the remaining ingredients and just before serving, stir into the hot curry.

▶ To serve, spoon over hot noodles or rice.

# GINGER LIME SYLLABUB

Syllabubs were immensely popular with the Elizabethans, but theirs were simply foamy drinks made by milking the cow straight into a cup or bowl of cider or wine – a kind of early alcoholic milk shake.

By the eighteenth century, however, the syllabub had become a more sophisticated creamy dessert with whipped cream and perhaps fruit juices. The traditional syllabub of this century is invariably flavoured with lemon, sherry and/or brandy.  My version uses the same classic technique, but the flavourings have taken on a tropical touch.

(SERVES 6)
juice of 2 limes
125 ml/4 fl oz green ginger
    wine
50 g/1¾ oz sugar
300 ml/10 fl oz double cream

*to garnish*
lime slices

▶ Put all the ingredients in a bowl and whisk to form soft peaks. (Don't worry about the amount of liquid, it will work.) Chill for up to 2 hours.

▶ To serve, divide between 6 chilled glasses and decorate with lime slices.

## Menu 6

# Lazy Laid-back Lunch or Dinner

Most of the preparation for this rather flashy menu is done well in advance, and even the lamb cooks itself unattended, leaving the cook free to hang loose.

# Roast Ham-wrapped Asparagus

 My favourite kind of starter. Not only does it taste wonderful, but can all be prepared in advance, kept in the fridge and just whacked in the oven at the last minute.

You could use Parma ham for this recipe but I think Serrano is far superior and is now available in most large supermarkets.

(serves 6)

1 kg/2¼ lb asparagus, bottom
⅓ cut away and discarded
12 slices Serrano ham (see
above)
extra virgin olive oil

*the dressing*
1 tbsp balsamic vinegar
4 tbsp extra virgin olive oil
2 tomatoes, peeled, deseeded
and chopped
salt and pepper

▶ Preheat the oven to 200°C/400°F/gas 6.

▶ Cook the asparagus in plenty of boiling salted water until 'al dente'. The time will depend on the thickness of the asparagus so you must keep testing it with the point of a knife, somewhere between 2 and 3 minutes probably. Drain, refresh in cold water, drain again and pat dry.

▶ Divide into 6 bundles and wrap each in 2 pieces of ham, leaving the tips exposed. Arrange on a lightly oiled baking sheet, drizzle with a little oil and bake for about 10 minutes or until the ham is beginning to brown and crisp slightly.

▶ Meanwhile, combine the dressing ingredients, seasoning to taste.

▶ To serve, put the parcels on 6 warm plates and drizzle the dressing in a circle around and over.

# Roast Lamb and Potatoes with Lemon, Garlic and Rosemary

This way of cooking lamb is Greek in influence – the sort of thing the village women took to the bakers to be cooked for Sunday lunch after the day's bread was baked.

Don't be nervous about the amount of garlic. The long cooking and the fact that the cloves are left whole will render them soft, buttery and mellow and your guests will be fighting for them, not avoiding them!

You will need a large oiled roasting tin or shallow ovenproof dish big enough to fit the lamb and the potatoes, without piling the potatoes on top of each other too much. Something which looks nice enough to bring to the table if possible as this recipe looks so wonderful when it comes out of the oven.

**(SERVES 6)**

'needles' from 4 sprigs rosemary (amount not crucial, but loads)

1 leg of lamb (approx. 1.35–1.8 kg/3–4 lb)

6 large waxy potatoes, each peeled, and cut into about 6 long wedges (about 1.35 kg/3 lb)

12 whole cloves garlic, peeled

300 ml/10 fl oz water

2 lemons

6 tbsp fruity extra virgin olive oil (1 tbsp for greasing the tin/dish)

salt and pepper

▶ Preheat the oven to 190°C/375°F/gas 5, and scatter half the rosemary over the bottom of the oiled baking tin or dish.

▶ Wipe the leg of lamb with kitchen paper, then sit it in the middle of the roasting tin/dish, surrounded by the potatoes and garlic. Pour over the water.

▶ Cut one of the lemons into 6 wedges, then cut these wedges in half across, and tuck these in among the potatoes and meat. Sprinkle the remaining rosemary on top. Squeeze the juice from the other lemon then drizzle this and the olive oil over everything. Season generously.

▶ Roast for 2 hours. Halfway through, baste the meat with any juices in the tin/dish and poke the potatoes about a bit (they will have shrunk slightly), bringing any pale surfaces to the top to brown.

▶ Leave the meat to rest in a warm place for about 15 minutes before serving. If at that stage you think the potatoes could be a bit browner, return them to the oven and turn the heat briefly up to full.

▶ Carve the meat and serve from the tin/dish, accompanied by one simple fresh green vegetable.

# Stir-fried Apples with Cinnamon, Currants and Brandy

Some people are surprised by the idea of stir-frying fruit, but it works brilliantly and produces a 'proper' pudding in minutes.

(SERVES 6)

75 g/2¾ oz currants

4 tbsp brandy

1 tbsp vegetable oil

25 g/1 oz unsalted butter

6 dessert apples, peeled, cored
    and each sliced into
        8 wedges at the last minute

2 tbsp brown sugar

1 tsp ground cinnamon

▶ Put the currants in a small container with the brandy, cover with food wrap and leave for at least 2 hours but preferably overnight to macerate (or zap for 1 minute on 100% in the microwave).

▶ Heat the oil and butter in a wok or large frying pan and stir-fry the apple wedges over a medium/high heat for 3–4 minutes or until beginning to soften.

▶ Add the sugar and cinnamon and continue to stir-fry until the apple slices begin to caramelise slightly, then add the currants and brandy and stir-fry for 1 more minute.

▶ Serve immediately with Greek-style yogurt, crème fraîche or vanilla ice cream.

# MENU 7
# DESIGNER DINNER

Designed to impress and delight, this swanky menu is produced with the absolute minimum of time and effort.

# ROAST CHERRY TOMATOES WITH GARLIC AND TWIGGY HERBS

 This is my second favourite recipe in the whole world as it produces such fabulous results with amazingly little effort. It is also a very posh recipe! It was given to me by my ex-boss, designer David Sassoon, who has made clothes for just about every royal, rich or famous woman you can think of . . . and in turn it was given to him by his sister, Lady Marguerite Woolf, so you can't get much posher than that. (I have adapted it slightly.)

By twiggy herbs I mean things like rosemary, thyme and bay leaves, which will stand up to roasting. Exact quantities don't matter, but you do need masses and they look so nice in the finished dish. Don't use less than 12 bay leaves, 12 sprigs thyme and 6 sprigs rosemary.

(SERVES 6)
650 g/1 lb 7 oz cherry tomatoes
lots of twiggy herbs (see
    above)
4 cloves garlic, chopped
6 tbsp extra virgin olive oil
salt and pepper

▶ Preheat the oven to 200°C/400°F/gas 6.

▶ Put the tomatoes, herbs, garlic and half the oil in a roasting tin or shallow ovenproof dish into which they fit quite snugly in one layer. Season well, toss all together and roast for about 30 minutes or until the tomatoes just begin to collapse slightly. Do not cook until they split.

▶ To serve, drizzle with the remaining oil and serve straight from the oven with crusty bread to mop up the juices.

# BACON-WRAPPED QUAILS ROASTED ON POLENTA

Most large supermarkets now sell quails and I like to keep some in my freezer for last-minute dinner parties. You do of course need to take them out in the morning to allow them to defrost properly.

Polenta is a 'meal' made from maize and whilst admittedly rather boring cooked just as it is, it is really good if you then cool it, slice it, brush it with olive oil and either grill or fry it until crispy. It tastes particularly good in this dish, where it has Parmesan added and is then cooked under the quails so that it becomes impregnated with all the wonderful juices which drip from the birds and the bacon. Make sure you buy the 'express' or 'instant' kind which only takes 5 minutes to cook.

(SERVES 6)

200 g/7 oz instant polenta
   (see above)
750 ml/27 fl oz water
salt and pepper
75 g/2¾ oz Parmesan cheese,
   freshly grated
extra virgin olive oil
6 quails
3 cloves garlic, cut in half
12 rashers streaky smoked
   bacon

▶ Preheat the oven to 220°C/425°F/gas 7.

▶ Cook the polenta in the water with salt according to the instructions on the packet. Season with pepper and add the Parmesan a minute or so before the cooking time is up.

▶ Oil 6 large Yorkshire pudding tins or small flan tins. Divide the cooked polenta between the tins and smooth the top with a knife. Brush the tops with more oil.

▶ Brush the quails lightly with oil, push ½ clove garlic into each cavity, and season with salt and pepper. Wrap each in two rashers of bacon and secure with wooden cocktail sticks.

▶ Sit the quails on to their little polenta 'rafts' and bake for about 30 minutes or until cooked through and the bacon crisped.

▶ To serve, remove the cocktail sticks and place each quail sitting on its crispy little polenta 'raft' in the centre of a hot plate, and surround with plainly cooked (steamed or boiled) fresh vegetables. Drizzle these with a little olive oil if you like, sprinkle with a little pepper, and serve immediately.

▲ Spicy Fish Soup. See page 115.

▲ Orange and Almond Salad with Rose Water. See page 116.

# Peaches in Pinot Noir

It is a French country tradition to simply take a peach from the fruit bowl at the end of the meal, and slice it into your last glass of red wine. It might seem more obvious to match fruit with white wine, but if you think of Sangria this combination makes sense.

Pinot Noir is the ideal wine because of its soft, mellow berry-like flavour but any soft fruity wine like a Beaujolais works very well.

(SERVES 6)

6 peaches

350 ml/12 fl oz red wine (see above)

2 tbsp warmed runny honey (I love lavender honey)

▶ Dip the peaches in boiling water for a few seconds. The skin should then slip off easily. Halve, remove the stones and slice.

▶ Put about a quarter of the wine in a bowl with the honey and whisk to dissolve, then add the rest of the wine and the sliced peaches.

▶ Chill for at least 4 hours or up to 24 for the flavours to develop.

▶ To serve, divide between 6 glasses and serve just as it is. (No need for cream or anything else.)

MENU 8

# YET ANOTHER TRIP AROUND THE WORLD

Although I spend a very pleasant percentage of my year travelling abroad and collecting ideas, inspirations and recipes from the different countries I visit, the recipes which I end up cooking at home are the ones which give the most impact with the minimum of effort. Particularly important are dishes which can be prepared well in advance like the first and last courses of this menu. When I invite people for a meal I like to spend as much time with them as possible, not isolated from them in the kitchen or giving a cookery demonstration!

## EGG PÂTÉ WITH 'CAVIAR'

This rich eggy pâté, inspired by an Australian recipe, makes an unusual and delicious start to the meal. It is also wonderfully quick and easy to make. The pâté can be made up to 24 hours in advance and kept in the fridge, but only add the 'caviar' at the last minute or the colour may 'bleed'.
If you are feeling very extravagant you could use salmon eggs (available from delicatessens and some large supermarkets) instead of the black lumpfish roe.

(SERVES 6 AS A FIRST COURSE)
6 hard-boiled large free-range
   eggs (size 1), finely chopped
6 spring onions (including good
   green parts), chopped
1 tbsp very finely chopped dill,
   tarragon or chervil
85 g/3 oz unsalted butter,
   melted
175 ml/6 fl oz fromage frais
salt and pepper
1 x 100 g jar black lumpfish roe

*to serve*
salad leaves
lemon wedges
herb sprigs

▶ In a bowl mix the chopped eggs, spring onions, herb, butter and 4 tbsp of the fromage frais. Season to taste with salt and pepper. Go steady on the salt as the lumpfish roe is quite salty.

▶ Spoon the mixture into a suitable serving dish. Chill for at least 4 hours or up to 24.

▶ Just before serving spread the remaining fromage frais over the egg mixture, then carefully spread the lumpfish roe over this, or arrange attractively in dollops.

▶ To serve, spoon on to plates and garnish with a few salad leaves, lemon wedges and sprigs of herbs.

# SPICY FISH SOUP

Many cooks are afraid of attempting fish soups, but most people love these light but nutritious one-dish meals when they try them in restaurants. This one has a definite Thai influence (one of my favourite cuisines), but takes only about 10–15 minutes to prepare and cook. Choose skinless firm white fish – monkfish, huss, halibut, turbot or haddock etc.

(SERVES 6)

1 tbsp vegetable oil

1 red or yellow pepper, deseeded and chopped

4 tbsp Thai green curry paste (see page 106)

1 x 400 ml tin coconut milk

1 litre/1¾ pt light chicken or fish stock (a cube is fine)

1 x 275 g tin sliced bamboo shoots, drained (supermarkets)

3 tbsp frozen peas

500 g/1 lb 2 oz skinless white fish (see above), cubed

300 g/10½ oz raw peeled large prawns

2 tbsp oriental fish sauce

juice of 1 lime (or more to taste)

*to serve*

3 spring onions, chopped

sliced fresh chilli

▶ Heat the oil in a large saucepan and stir-fry the pepper for about 5 minutes over a medium heat or until beginning to soften.

▶ Stir in the curry paste, followed by the coconut milk and, when amalgamated, the stock. Bring to the boil and turn down the heat.

▶ Add the bamboo shoots, peas, fish and prawns and simmer for 2–3 minutes or until the fish is just cooked through. Do not overcook or the fish will fall apart and the prawns become rubbery.

▶ Add the fish sauce and lime juice to taste.

▶ Serve in heated bowls, scattered with chopped spring onions and chilli slices (to taste).

# ORANGE AND ALMOND SALAD WITH ROSE WATER

A lovely simple but exotic tasting end to an unusual meal.
Rose water is available from delicatessens and the baking section of large supermarkets.

**(SERVES 6)**

**6–9 oranges (depending on size)**

**75 g/2¾ oz toasted flaked almonds**

**1 heaped tbsp caster sugar (or to taste)**

**1-2 tbsp rose water (see above), or to taste**

*to garnish*
**mint leaves**

▶ Peel and slice the oranges across thinly and arrange attractively on a platter.

▶ Scatter over the almonds, sprinkle with the sugar and then the rose water and chill for at least 4 hours or overnight for the flavours to develop.

▶ Serve just as it is or with Greek-style yogurt.

# MENU 9
# MEDITERRANEAN MAGIC

A splendid vegetarian feast (except for the anchovies) based on a collection of recipes inspired by the sunny cooking of the Med.

# GRILLED FENNEL WITH LEMON AND OLIVE OIL

 This crunchy, faintly aniseed-tasting vegetable is available from good greengrocers and large supermarkets. Generally used raw in salads it is also delicious cooked. It can be cooked under a preheated grill, on a hot ridged heavy iron 'grill' frying pan or, best of all, over glowing charcoal.

(SERVES 6)
4 bulbs fennel, trimmed,
    cleaned and cut lengthways
    into 1 cm/¹/₂ in slices
extra virgin olive oil
juice of 1 lemon
salt and pepper (Maldon salt
    and coarsely cracked pepper
    are best)

*to serve*
lemon wedges

▶ Brush the fennel slices lightly with olive oil and grill for 3–4 minutes on each side or until just beginning to char a little.

▶ To serve, divide between 6 hot plates and drizzle with the lemon juice and a little olive oil. Sprinkle with salt and pepper to taste and serve with lemon wedges and good bread to mop up the delicious juices.

# Pissaladière

I have a wonderful gas barbecue called an Outdoor Chef (available from large stores and garden centres) which has a lid and gets very hot thus making the best thin and crispy pizzas in the world. So long as you roll out the dough thinly enough, an ordinary domestic oven, preheated as hot as it will go, will provide excellent results.

With this, my favourite simple topping – of slow-cooked onions, anchovies and olives – pizza becomes a pissaladière, a classic dish from the South of France. You will need to cook the pizzas in batches (although you can cook the first two together, see below), and eat them as they are done.

(SERVES 6)

*the dough*
500 g/1 lb 2 oz plain flour
1 sachet 'fast-action yeast'
1 tsp salt
3 tsp olive oil
300 ml/10 fl oz hand-hot water

*the topping*
4 tbsp extra virgin olive oil
6 onions, thinly sliced
salt and pepper
2 x 55 g tins anchovies, drained
    and halved
about 36 pitted black olives

▶ First make the dough. Place the flour in a bowl with the yeast and salt. Stir in the oil and hot water and bring the mixture together to form a ball of dough.

▶ Knead the dough for a good 10 minutes, place in an oiled bowl, cover with kitchen film and leave to rise in a warm place for 1–2 hours or until doubled in size.

▶ Preheat the oven to 240°C/475°F/gas 9 or as hot as it will go.

▶ Meanwhile heat the oil in a large lidded saucepan, and add the onions and about ½ tsp salt. Stir thoroughly to combine then cook, covered, over the lowest possible heat (a heat diffuser is indispensable) for an hour, stirring occasionally, or until the onions have melted down into a very soft mass (but not browned).

▶ Remove the risen dough from the bowl, knead for 1–2 minutes, then divide it into 3 equal parts. Roll these out on a floured surface to make 3 large roughly rectangular shapes. Place on 3 lightly oiled baking sheets.

▶ Spread the onions over the pizza bases then scatter with the anchovies and olives. Season with salt and pepper and drizzle over a little extra oil.

▶ Bake for 15 minutes (see above) or until the base is crisp. Cook 2 first, and switch them top to bottom in the oven halfway through. Then cook the third one.

▶ To serve, cut up the pizzas as soon as they come out of the oven and serve with the following pepper dish.

▶ Eat immediately!

# Braised Peppers with Mint

I love this way of cooking peppers. It is so much simpler than the grilling and peeling method, and I think the result is just as tasty. The sweetness of the slow-cooked peppers is set off perfectly by the sharpness of the lemon juice and the tang of the mint.
Unless you have a very large lidded sauté pan or wok, I think it is best to cook the peppers in two separate pans.

(SERVES 6)

6 tbsp extra virgin olive oil
10 red or yellow peppers, deseeded and cut into large bite-sized pieces
salt and pepper
juice of 2 lemons
5 heaped tbsp chopped mint

▶ Divide the oil between 2 large lidded saucepans (see above), divide the peppers between them, season well with salt and pepper, then cook, tightly covered, over the lowest heat possible (heat diffusers are invaluable) for 1 hour, shaking the pan occasionally or until the peppers are meltingly tender. Transfer to a large serving bowl and allow to cool.

▶ Stir in the lemon juice and chopped mint just before serving.

# BANANAS IN COINTREAU AND LEMON

I think bananas are a very much underrated fruit, which somehow seem to be associated mainly with children. I enjoyed this very 'adult' pudding at a wonderful restaurant called Wolfe's Den in the Ligurian hills of Northern Italy. The yogurt is my addition. You can of course serve it with cream, fromage frais, vanilla ice cream or just as it is.

(SERVES 6)

6 bananas

juice of 1 lemon

5 tbsp Cointreau (or other
    orange-flavoured liqueur)

2 tbsp sugar

*to serve*
Greek-style yogurt

▶ Peel the bananas and slice diagonally. Place in a bowl and pour over the lemon juice and Cointreau, then sprinkle over the sugar.

▶ Carefully and gently toss the bananas so that each piece is coated in the liquid. (Hands are the best implement for this job.) Chill for 30–60 minutes.

▶ Serve chilled with Greek-style yogurt.

## MENU 10

# A FABULOUS FEAST OF FISH

Although effortless and extremely healthy, this fishy feast is packed with flavour and very satisfying to eat.

## SEVICHE AND AVOCADO SALAD

 Based on a classic South American dish, the raw fish in this recipe is 'cooked' by the lime juice. It is essential for the success of this dish to use only the freshest of fish. If you don't like the idea of eating 'raw' fish substitute the same quantity of cooked shelled prawns and proceed with the same method of preparation.

The amount of chilli given here is only a guideline as different types vary in 'heat' and you might want to add more or less.

(SERVES 6)

500 g/1 lb 2 oz skinless firm white fish fillets (see method)

175 ml/6 fl oz fresh lime juice (the juice of 6–8 limes)

1 large tomato (or 2 small),

6 spring onions

2 fresh chillies (according to taste, see above)

3 tbsp finely chopped fresh coriander

3 tbsp extra virgin olive oil

1/2 tsp salt

1 tsp sugar

Tabasco sauce (optional)

to serve

2 ripe avocado pears

about 1/2 x 200 g packet prepared mixed leaves

▶ Use turbot, halibut, haddock, monkfish or cod, etc. Cut into 2cm/3/4 in cubes.

▶ Put the fish cubes into a non-metallic bowl and pour over the lime juice. Mix well. Cover with kitchen film and leave to marinate and 'cook' in the fridge for about 2–3 hours or until the fish has turned opaque looking.

▶ Meanwhile, finely chop the tomato (skinning it first if you can be bothered).

▶ Thinly slice the spring onions, including the good green parts.

▶ Deseed the fresh chillies, and chop them finely.

▶ Drain the fish in a sieve and catch the lime juice in a bowl.

▶ Put the fish in another bowl and mix with the tomato, spring onion, chillies, coriander, oil, salt and sugar. Mix thoroughly and chill for about another 30 minutes.

▶ Taste the mixture, and if you think you would like a bit more 'heat' add a few drops of Tabasco sauce and mix thoroughly.

▶ Meanwhile cut the avocado pears in half and remove the skin and stones. Cut the flesh across into approximately 5 mm/¼ in slices and place in the bowl with the lime juice. Mix thoroughly but gently so that each piece is coated. This will prevent discoloration. Strain off and discard the lime juice. Return the bowl to the fridge until needed.

▶ To serve, arrange 'nests' of leaves on 6 large plates. Mound the avocado slices in the middle of these, and the chilled fish mixture on top of the avocado. Serve immediately.

# SALMON EN PAPILLOTE

 Cooking fish by this method is not only simple and foolproof, providing perfectly cooked fish with the minimum fuss and kitchen smells, but is also ideal for entertaining as the packages can be prepared several hours in advance and kept on a baking sheet in the fridge, ready to be popped in the oven at the last moment. It is also incredibly low in calories.

(SERVES 6)

6 salmon portions, fillet or
    steaks, each weighing
    approx. 200 g/7 oz
salt and pepper
400 g/14 oz frozen petits pois,
    thawed
12 fresh dill sprigs or 6 tsp
    chopped parsley
6 thin slices lemon
6 tsp extra virgin olive oil

▶ Preheat the oven to 220°C/425°F/gas 7. Cut 6 circles of greaseproof paper or baking parchment (you can use kitchen foil but it doesn't look quite as pretty for serving), each measuring approximately 40 cm/15 in across. Fold each one in half and open out flat again.

▶ Season each salmon portion lightly with salt and pepper and place on one half of the paper circles, about 2.5 cm/1 in away from the crease. Pile on the peas (some will spill around the fish), top with the herb and a lemon slice and season again lightly with salt and pepper. Drizzle the oil over the top. Fold the other half of the paper circle over to cover the filling and then twist and fold the two curved edges together, like a pie crust to completely seal the parcels.

▶ Arrange the parcels in one layer, not touching, on a lightly greased baking sheet (or 2 if necessary) and bake for 12 minutes. Then remove from the oven and allow to 'rest' for another 2–3 minutes before serving.

▶ To serve, place the parcels on 6 heated plates, cut a cross in the top of each with a pair of scissors and serve immediately with simply cooked new potatoes and grilled tomato halves (spread each half first with a little crushed garlic).

# RUM, RAISIN AND COCONUT TART

I love coconut in both sweet and savoury recipes and most supermarkets sell it in solidified block form called 'creamed coconut' which looks somewhat like a hard block of lard. This is an excellent product and is very pure.

(SERVES 6–8)

*the pastry*

175 g/6 oz plain flour
25 g/1 oz desiccated coconut
115 g/4 oz unsalted butter
1 heaped tbsp caster sugar
1 free-range egg, lightly beaten, plus 1 white for glazing

*the filling*

50 g/1¾ oz raisins soaked in 4 tbsp dark rum for 3 hours or overnight
150 ml/5 fl oz single cream
1 x 200 g block creamed coconut, roughly chopped
150 ml/5 fl oz milk
3 free-range eggs, lightly beaten
1 heaped tbsp sugar

▶ Make the pastry. Put the flour and desiccated coconut in a mixing bowl and rub in the butter until the mixture resembles fine breadcrumbs. Stir in the sugar. Mix in the egg and, working quickly, bring the mixture together until it forms a smooth dough. Alternatively make it in a food processor. Wrap in plastic wrap and chill for 30 minutes before using. Preheat the oven to 220°C/425°F/gas 7.

▶ Roll the dough out thinly and use to line a loose-bottomed 26 cm/10½ in metal flan tin. Prick the bottom here and there with a fork and bake blind for 5 minutes. Remove from the oven and brush all over with the egg white. Return to the oven for another 5 minutes. This will provide a waterproof coating and prevent the pastry going soggy on the bottom when the liquid filling is added. Turn the oven down to 190°C/375°F/gas 5.

▶ Meanwhile heat the cream and creamed coconut together in a small pan, stirring constantly, just until the coconut has dissolved. Remove from the heat and stir in the cold milk, followed by the eggs. Tip the raisins into a sieve over the saucepan so that any rum falls into the coconut mixture. Stir this in. Spread the raisins over the bottom of the pastry case and pour in the coconut mixture. Bake for about 30 minutes or until the filling has set and the top is nicely browned. Allow to cool.

▶ Serve at room temperature with whipped cream if you are feeling lavish, or some slices of tropical fruit for a marginally less calorific pud.

# INDEX